BADGER STATE

A Wisconsin Memoir

BADGER STATE

A Wisconsin Memoir

KATHLEEN McDONOUGH MUNDO

Henschel HAUS
publishing, inc.
Milwaukee, Wisconsin

Published by HenschelHAUS Publishing, Inc.
www.henschelHAUSbooks.com

ISBN (paperback): 978159598-787-7
ISBN (hardcover): 978159598-788-4
E-ISBN: 978159598-789-1
LCCN: 2020943663

Cover design and layout by MAD Studios, Miami, FL.

*The cover photo was taken by the author in December 2017 along
Duck Lake Nature Trail in Lake Geneva, Wisconsin. The image
includes the author's daughter, Isabel, and the family's Labrador
Retriever, Winston.*

Printed in the United States of America.

For Isabel, Michael, Caroline,
and John

If I know what love is, it is because of you.
—Hermann Hesse

Table of Contents

The Move

*"I spent a lot of time looking for your birthday card
and it says all the things I wanted to say.
You've been a wonderful daughter to me
and I appreciate it."*

"You've been a wonderful mom and I appreciate it."

"Well, I don't know...but I did my best."

*"That's all anyone can ask of anyone in this world.
To do their best."*

WHEN I WAS SIX YEARS OLD, our family packed up the station wagon and our olive-green Ford Pinto and headed across the "Cheddar Curtain" from a Chicago suburb to Racine, Wisconsin. As the youngest of six children, I was usually the one crammed in the back of the car along with our massive fawn-colored Great Dane, Sam.

I absolutely loved that dog, but hated the Pinto. It was an unappealing, murky shade of weird both inside and out, and was way too small for our family, even as a second car. It always smelled like gasoline and seemed to have no ventilation. Every little bump or stop by the driver meant my head banged up against the glass along the hatchback.

Later, it was learned that the most minor of accidents involving the Pinto could lead to large explosions and horrifyingly gruesome personal injuries due to questionable gas tank placement. I'm not sure whether this sort of information would have made any difference in my "back seat" arrangement—safety is expensive, after all—and we never had a lot of extra money around and besides, what were the odds someone would get hurt, anyway?

We were a family embarking toward a new frontier. There were ten years between oldest and youngest in our lineup: Tim, Margie, John, Pat, Morgan, and me. It seemed like there were more of us, and yet, sometimes, it seemed like everyone was missing.

To a kid, moving away from your first home for the first time is a very big deal. To a kid, moving from the Chicago suburbs to Racine, Wisconsin was like being transported to another country. It changed our lives and our family structure forever. Some of us would stay, some would leave sooner than expected, and some of us would try to work our way back and forth, following the family move to the Badger State in the year of our nations' bicentennial celebration, 1976.

The Place

WISCONSIN IS A BEAUTIFULLY underrated Mid-western state. Anyone who is not from Wisconsin thinks it's all about cows and farms and beer and cheese and things that are Germanic or Scandinavian in culture. There's no denying it; a lot of it is. You can experience fantastically delicious fried cheese curds and Friday-night fish fries featuring icy cold Old Fashioned cocktails—bourbon-based, of course, not whiskey, ever, of course—where just about everything from the fish to the potatoes to the bread is deep-fried.

Friday-night fish fry indulgences are typically followed by Saturday morning Bloody Mary orders at the local tavern, with as many salty and briny garnishes that can fit: olives, pickles, cheddar cheese cubes, and celery, with a beer shot chaser.

Countless brands of craft beers eclipse the wine varieties at liquor and grocery stores, including some brews that can only be bought in Wisconsin, produced in little towns that look like cute European hamlets. Acres upon acres of idyllic farm fields with corn and soybeans and cabbage and all sorts of other indistinguishable crops march in tidy rows of gold and green that seem to go on forever from early spring through late fall.

There are fields upon endless pastures sprinkled with every combination of black and white and tan cows that you can imagine. Wisconsin is home to more than 8,000 dairy farms, imposing and glorious big red barns, tall gray silos topped with shiny silver, green grasses, and sparkling blue lakes throughout. The state is rightfully proud of the fact that it houses the second largest number of organic farms in the country. Badger State farmers are hard-working and unassuming and honest and just plain good, above all.

And while Racine County in Southeastern Wisconsin does have many, if not most, of those things within its four corners, the county and the city are unique in many ways.

First, the city of Racine is just about an hour north of Chicago, with Lake Michigan on its eastern border. There are those with a full appreciation of the fact that the "Great Lakes" are, in fact, very "great" and large. And yet visitors will without fail stand in front of Lake Michigan for the first time, dumbfounded by the fact that "you can't see across it … it looks just like an ocean without all that salt!"

Second, Racine is bordered by Milwaukee to the north and the city of Kenosha to the south.

Third, to the west, Racine is made up of crop, dairy, and livestock farms that don't look at all like the small downtown area, which hints of what things must have looked like 150 years ago in its old buildings and churches. In many ways, this means country meets city and city meets suburbs within a fairly small area, though not always in the most agreeable way.

The city of Racine happens to be home to more than 75,000 inhabitants from very different walks of life, cultures, colors, beliefs, and religions. Some people who have grown up in the town, or who have looked at it from the outside, think it's a place where racism abides, but that was never really my experience. That said, many will surely disagree after having experienced a much different lifestyle than my own.

While much of the county grew up on and continues to focus on farming, Racine also hosts a respectable manufacturing industry and a much lesser tourist industry. People who visit it seem to realize its potential and beauty, while those who live there go on with their everyday lives as if the future of the town will happen on its own.

Some people associate the state's nickname with an oversized mammal wearing a striped red -and-white sweater, or Bucky Badger, the team mascot for the University of Wisconsin. In reality, Wisconsin came to be known as the Badger State as a result of groups of zinc and lead miners in the early 1800s, who came to the state looking for new opportunities, much like our family did one hundred and fifty years later. Legend has it that the miners often dug caves into the sides of mines for shelter, as did real-life badgers.

The place we moved to is not like every other Wisconsin city. It has it all—without knowing it. After World War II, Eastern European immigrants and southern-born African Americans came to Racine as part of the Great Migration to join the largely German, Swedish, and Danish Lutheran farming communities. Their hope was to find high-paying factory jobs, because most of the agriculture in the state was tied up by families who passed the family farm down from one generation to the next.

The world of industry was another story. With the city's close proximity to both Milwaukee and Chicago and its prime location on Lake Michigan, large manufacturing companies like S.C. Johnson and J.I. Case, the tractor company, needed employees to power their factories.

Eventually, many planned on buying homes of their own and raising families, which many of these pioneers did. Moms and dads went to work in places where they made things like soaps, shampoos, and mosquito repellant, as well as garbage disposals and tractors. People made a good living and went home at dinner time. They were actually able to explain to their kids what they did at work.

Though not as glamorous as finance or banking or other service industries, Racine offered work that produced tangible items you could put your hands on and be proud of, even if you were merely a small part of the process.

Most kids growing up in Racine, like the ones in our family, would have absolutely no clue or care in the world about these sort of things. Kids generally don't care about the histories of those around them, because the younger you are, the less history you have. The present and the future are the riches of the young. Most come to learn and appreciate important facts like these over the years as they get older and develop a perspective that only comes from living different experiences. With age, we develop a greater ability to see the forest beyond the trees.

Our family's move to Racine meant taking six kids out of grade school, middle school, and high school, where just about every single one of those kids was seemingly in a perfectly happy place, to then start over with a completely new life, new schools and new friends. Surely our parents, Tom and Jackie, talked about the move and thought the opportunity to be a good one. Well, maybe. Whether they fully vetted the change in scenery, versus what actually occurred on the likely more impulsive side of the decision -making continuum, will never be known.

It was the mid-1970s, and the rest of the world of American teenagers and twenty-somethings was busy being or imitating hippies, reeling from a soul-crushing war, and doing whatever the hell they wanted to do instead of being told what they had to do.

Our parents were living life on figurative roller skates, in the middle of holding down the fort amidst an "epidemic of kids," as our dad used to tell perfect strangers he'd just met.

Dad had recently taken a job offer as the General Manager of the Racine Country Club, which may have been a big deal to some, maybe by Wisconsin standards even, but it wasn't really. The job meant enough money to get our parents to move across the state line, but it would be decades before the era of television shows glorified hospitality and restaurant management. Back then, things were pretty much limited to Julia Child's cooking show and a few other random hospitality-type programs, and those didn't really appeal to kids, teens, or twenty-somethings.

The move was about money, not ego.

2932 Northwestern Avenue

WHILE THE JOURNEY MIGHT HAVE seemed like an eternity to a little kid sitting in the hatchback of a Pinto, it was only about an hour's drive north from Chicago. Somehow, though, it seemed as if moving to Wisconsin put us in a state of perpetual jetlag. For years, it felt as though something was always just a bit off; things just didn't feel quite right. The number of collective changes to the daily routine of our family all at once was massive to my seven-year-old self. New town, new home, new rooms, new things, new schools. It was a lot of new, all at once.

2932 Northwestern Avenue was to become our new house. It would not be our house for as long as we wanted, but as for this "new" home, our parents —well, our mom really—picked a beautiful, but very old Tudor Style home with a great big yard, directly across the street from our dad's new job at the Racine Country Club. It seemed ideal in terms of location and size, within easy walking distance to a few public schools and a Catholic school, assuming the weather wasn't too bad. Which was a really big assumption.

The house needed a pretty substantial amount of work and was a bit of a stretch for our family financially. In a way, it represented hope and achievement and the things our family hoped that we would become. Ultimately, the necessary projects and work in the house remained undone but probably were not that important anyway. It may not have dawned on anyone that this was a large reason why it had been on the market for so long. In a way, the house was a bit of a loner in the neighborhood. Most of the houses were smaller and so they fit smaller families better. In this part of town and largely throughout the county, big families like ours were a bit of an anomaly.

We all fell in love with that house immediately. It was an old house at the time, built around the turn of the century, but it was brand new to us. It felt like it had a personality, a bit haughty and proud and aware of the fact that it was the star of the block even if it did have its share of bumps and bruises. It didn't care that it was aging because its beauty overshadowed its other issues. It had stairs and turns and rooms and corners in places you'd never expect. The house alone kept most of the six kids from wandering off.

As each of us got older, we had distinct memories about that house. Some of us even found the house popping up in our dreams as a metaphorical representations of childhood, youth, or our family.

Memories are built around the premise of a strange phenomenon. You think you remember everything, or maybe you remember very little. In reality, it's the unusual you are most likely to recall, not the everyday. That stuff just blends in and becomes background noise. Sometimes certain events really stand out because they were so very different from the normal routine. Other times, maybe it was just something so jarring or emotional or just plain odd about a memory that puts it out on an island in your mind—far away from other long, common, repetitive, monotonous days.

Looking back, it seems almost impossible to sort out some old memories from others—the typical from the unusual, the everyday from the unique. None of us would remember the monotony of getting up day after day to drag ourselves to school. But we remembered when snowstorms and subzero temperatures came, making the walk to school treacherous in makeshift snow boots lined with nothing but recycled plastic bread bags to keep the wet snow from seeping in.

We would forget the daily meals and routines, but remember the beautiful holiday celebrations orchestrated by our mom. Even when we didn't have a lot, which was most of the time, she refused to give up on making holidays memorable in every possible way.

15

This house, though, it was special. It stayed with us, and maybe it had something to do with the fact that we would have to leave it much sooner than we expected or even wanted. The house was a great big, living, breathing being full of mystery and adventure.

We knew little about it, although there was some talk about it once having been the home of William Horlick, the inventor of malted milk who moved from England to Racine in the late 1880s. After creating the product, he started the Horlick Malted Milk Company and moved to Chicago. Fortunately for Racine factory workers, production of the malted milk remained in Racine at the Horlick plant down the street.

Our house was nice, but not that nice. It had great bones, but much of the interior was terribly dated. Still, the stories about our home's prior owners made for good discussion around the dinner table and without a website to refute it at the time, stories went untested. Whatever Horlick's time spent in Racine, he made an impression and one of the city's largest public high schools was named after him. We believed it had to have been owned by someone important, whether Horlick himself or an executive, because it made us feel important to live in it.

We learned much later that the home had been owned by the Cushmans, a family who bore little to no similarities to ours. A Cushman from an earlier generation invented technology that helped develop the first telephone. Dr. Cushman was working for a telegraph company, testing wires in western Racine when he inadvertently discovered sounds—in this case, a croaking frog—could be transmitted via wires over ten miles away. Dr. Cushman challenged Alexander Graham Bell in federal court in Chicago, but eventually lost, though he made a fortune in royalties on various components and inventions. As it happened, his son inhabited our home with his own family, earning enough in ongoing royalties to never have to work.

The house even had a butler's pantry and pretty much no one in our town was known to have any servants, not even the fancy executives at S.C. Johnson Wax living on the north side of town along the lakefront. The butler's pantry connected our kitchen to the dining room with a long passageway. Under the carpeting sat a raised buzzer—a "butler's bell"—that rang in the butler's pantry when you pressed down on it with your foot.

One Christmas, excited about Santa's upcoming visit, the smaller kids in the family over-buzzed and managed to kill the butler bell for good. Fixing it meant cutting up and replacing carpet, topped with an electrician's bill and well, and that would have been a great big "nope" from the management department, also known as our mom.

In the winter, which seemed to be the longest of the seasons by far, the house never got warm enough. On bitter-cold Wisconsin winter days, the cat food and water dishes kept in the hallway by the back door leading to the garage would freeze.

Other things about the house: You could never flush a toilet without the water continuing to run until you "jiggled" the handle. Since no one in the family was especially handy, things that were broken tended to stay that way for a while. This would annoy most people but in our house, eventually you got used to things being broken and you found another way or at some point you just didn't notice it anymore. A handyman was for emergencies, like the time someone attempted a home hot-water radiator repair job and instead, ended up with a very broken radiator, hot water pouring down the stairs in waves, all the way down into our basement, on a very cold winter day.

Just in front of 2932 on the funeral home side stood a fairly typical mailbox, which is normally a harmless thing not worth mentioning. But it became important much later. Ours was nothing special in appearance, silver-colored on a wooden pole with a red metal flag you put up to get your mail taken away if the mail carrier was paying attention that day.

Our mailbox was placed right next to a telephone pole, and always seemed to get knocked down and smashed each winter by wayward cars sliding on the icy and snowy street that curved in front of our house. We would be having dinner or playing in the snow in the backyard and would hear the tell-tale sign of a crack followed by a loud bam, which meant the mailbox went flying and it was time to stick it back on the pole or in some cases, buy a new one. No one in our house planned the location or thought to move it to a new spot, although the placement of the telephone pole was the real problem.

The front yard was a decent size, with much larger side and backyards, all for our private enjoyment. A small walkway led to the front door, which in warmer months was surrounded by lush, hanging English Ivy vines. For us, the yard seemed to go on for days, though in a visit as an adult, like most things, it didn't seem quite so large. The yard was home to thousands of perennials, from tulips to crocuses to lilies to violets that came out in a colorful shower of spring each year. Fruit trees from green apple to pear to plum dotted the huge backyard.

Entering the front of the house, you encountered a staircase leading to a landing with another set of stairs going down to the kitchen at a perfect right angle. Continuing up the stairs to the right were a few more stairs, which led to four bedrooms: two on the left divided by a bathroom, and two on the right. The house was old and of course the stairs and floors creaked, which made it very hard to sneak up on anyone.

Our parents had their own room, of course, which also happened to have the only air conditioner in the house. If we were quiet—and only if it was unbearably hot, as in the 95-degrees-plus zone—we were allowed to bring our pillows and covers into their room to sleep on the floor. Overall, we didn't have many memories of being too hot; usually we were freezing in the winter.

Next to our parent's room was a large bedroom with built-in bookcases and drawers in the closets, with a huge picture window overlooking the backyard. For some reason, three of my brothers—Tim (16), Pat (12), and Morgan (9) —were to share the large room. But the third oldest, John (14), had his own room across the hallway. Next to his was my room, which I shared with my sister Margie (15). I was seven years old.

Though the layout didn't make a lot of sense for our family, it worked. We could have stayed a lifetime, but didn't. In years to come, the house would at some point be converted into a law firm, and eventually, a hair salon and spa in which massage therapists set up shop in what used to be my bedroom.

Fighting Boredom
in Racine

As we grew up, when other friends were busy or it was too early or too late or too snowy or too cold to get to a friend's house, my brother Morgan was my perpetual playmate and enemy and best friend all in one. He was just eighteen months older than me, and it had to be a terrible disappointment to be squarely in your toddler days when another baby came along in the family. We played and fought and even though he regularly got the better of me when it came to physical altercations, I always forgave him because he was always there and it was better to have him around than playing alone.

We kids searched the entire house for ways to create our own entertainment. At the top of our house was an oddly designed, lofty, old attic, accessible only through our parents' bedroom. It was a weird set-up, because it wasn't like one of those attics you can only get to with a ladder or by pulling down a string attached to a pull-up staircase. This attic had a door you opened before walking through a hallway to get to our parents' bathroom. Once the creaky, old, yellow-painted door was opened, a crazy steep climb up a set of stairs took you into the attic itself.

The ascent was for the adventurous and the brave. Once you made it up, a long series of tiny, different rooms and compartments and places to explore appeared, even though it was almost always too hot to play up in the attic, thanks to the house's woefully inadequate energy efficiency. Morgan and I would sneak up to the attic to hide or play or spend long, boring days. We wandered all around the house, which had a surprising number of hidden cupboards and corridors for any games our collective imagination could create.

We set up indoor picnics with awful and amazing junk food combinations like Twinkies and Ding Dongs with sour cream and onion potato chips, or coconut-raspberry coated "Snowball" cakes with nuclear orange Cheetos or Okey-Dokey cheese popcorn that we'd buy with our spare change down the street at the Open Pantry convenience store. When we were bored—and we were a lot—we'd walk or bike down to the "OP" just to have a different place to hang out. It was never very busy so we could stop and talk to the cashier.

One year, the convenience store owners decided to put in a huge glass tub of water with a shot glass at the bottom. If you were able to get a quarter into that shot glass, you'd get a free Slushy, which was nothing more than crushed ice plus sugar plus artificial color. This became a carnival game of sorts, but seemingly as impossible as a claw game at a video arcade. We brought as many quarters as we could find, day after day after day, to try our hand at a chance at a free Slushy. It was nothing exciting, really, but the competition in all of us had the neighborhood kids hanging around and using pennies and nickels for practice.

Hours and hours of intense focus later, the neighborhood kids figured it out. Spin the quarter directly over the top of a shot glass, as fast as you could. And down it continued to spin, floating directly into the shot glass. Magic. The cashier, just as bored as we were, and not much older than sixteen, laughed and laughed while she served up one free Slushy after another. The owners found out the little neighborhood punks weren't so profitable after all, and soon the game was gone and we were back looking for things to do at our house.

Beneath the house was a basement that really was more of a musty, old, industrial-like cellar. It would have been perfect for storing wine, if anyone had actually imbibed in our house. The basement didn't seem to fit with the rest of our house. There were all sorts of rooms of different sizes and configurations that were connected without any meaningful rhyme or reason. At some point in history, the maze of rooms must have had a logical purpose; it just didn't make sense to us.

The basement had an ice-cold cement floor, nothing fancy, with rooms we used to store our winter clothes and other things, and also to keep with purposes unknown to the new owners. The cellar always smelled of mildew, even during the warmest and driest of days. One room was furnished with a washing machine and dryer, along with an old fold-out table that contained eight different piles of clothing, representing each of the inhabitants of the home.

While our mom did the laundry, if you wanted your clean clothes, you had better go down and get them yourself. This ended up in a war of wills with the younger brothers, who really didn't care much at all about how clean their clothes looked. They were just going to get dirty anyway.

Putting the clothes away is where our mom understandably drew the line. If you wanted to actually wear those clean clothes any time soon, you'd better make a trip down to the cellar. The boys saw this as implied approval to wear the same clothing for days on end.

Outside, just next to the side yard, was an empty lot that apparently came with the big house. In its early days, the lot became a garden with dozens of tomato plants, beans, and sunflowers. Our mom later got an offer to purchase the lot which, true to form, she stubbornly turned down. "It was ours and maybe we did need the money, but you can't have that land." The garden was even blessed by the new young priest over at our school, Father Mike from Sacred Heart Church. Plants and vegetables grew at an incredible pace that first summer, whether through the grace of God or the nutrient-rich soil or both.

We canned enough tomatoes to last longer than any of our high school careers. Later, the same lot would become an overgrown jungle of weeds and dead bushes. But while things were alive and growing all over the place, Morgan and I would run around the garden and hide and play between the lanes of tomato plants and sunflowers. There was no tomorrow to worry about. Life was perfect. For reasons unknown, a pigeon decided to set up shop in that garden for the summer and joined us while we played. We named him "Sunny."

We were Irish in a family that lacked sports and structure and direction, so with what seemed like endless summer days or nights and weekends with limited homework either assigned or completed, drinking in Wisconsin was bound to happen. You just got bored. And just about every kid had an older brother or sister willing to score them some beer, because their older siblings did it for them, and on and on.

The boys decided to build a fort outside where all of this could happen within yards of the house. Well, they were allowed or they just went ahead and did it; the facts aren't too clear on that. They went out into the neighborhood, scouring construction sites and dumpsters, picking up loose scraps of wood and metal and ended up building what might now be called a "tiny house." It had four walls and a roof, along with a vent on the top for smoke to get through, and seated anywhere from six to ten bodies.

My brothers hung out in the fort for hours at a time, mostly smoking weed. There was never a shortage of neighborhood kids hanging out in the fort and why wouldn't there be—it was like an apartment for teenagers. There were friends like Matt Leskowitz, John Fisher, and Scott Johnson. In high school, they'd later be known as burnouts because they either smoked cigarettes or weed, just like John, Pat, and Morgan. Still, they were nice guys who really didn't steal or do anything to hurt anyone else, and each of them was clever and likeable in his own right, so it was hard not to like them.

The guys were nice to me and my family and were around the house almost all the time. I'd even try to find a reason to hang out with my brothers' friends, since the parents of my female friends rarely allowed them to come to my house, with all those boys around. I'd make brownies or cookies and deliver them to the fort and they would let me hang out for five minutes or so, until they realized they couldn't talk trash or smoke weed around me and they gave me the boot.

We played countless games of hide-and-seek in the yard and the adjacent lot, though hide-and-seek can only go so far. With widely unstructured summer days ahead of us, our mom was under siege. "I'm bored!" "What's there to do?" Such queries were met with the same answer, every single time: "Go outside and play."

As the boys got older, they found ways to collect old junker cars, setting up shop in our garage. John was especially good at fixing cars, although he was completely self-taught. One day, one of them bought an old, beat-up Volkswagen Beetle. It was an absolute bucket of bolts. Not even John, who could fix just about any car, bothered with this one, and it ran for a couple of days at best. After that, they did the most logical thing. They waited for the parents to leave, and pushed it around the backyard, putting on a demolition derby with a group of friends. They took hammers and pieces of wood and whatever they could find, spending an entire day just beating the tar out of an inanimate object like absolute idiots who magically, like many times, did not suffer even a scratch.

In those days, kids could wander at large, whether in our backyard, down the street, at a neighbor's, in a quietly deserted schoolyard, or if we could find a family willing to take us to the lake—even better. As long as we were home around dinnertime, things were ok, and it didn't seem as though there was ever a thought to one of us failing to return.

The School & the Church

THOSE OF US STILL IN GRADE SCHOOL at the time of the move ended up at Sacred Heart School, a little under a mile away from our house, and a straight shot down Northwestern Avenue, past the Country Club, past the fire station, past the art museum, past the medical clinic, past a few apartment buildings and homes, past Gilmour, the free public middle school with the huge front yard, and past the old grain elevator where local farmers brought their wheat and corn for processing and distribution. Suddenly, you'd see the church that was shaped like a flying saucer, and just beyond it, Sacred Heart School.

Transferring into Sacred Heart School in the very middle of first grade was an especially traumatic event for me. It hit all of the "memory factors." The school and class were different than my old school, emotionally jarring, and the sort of event a kid will never forget because twenty-nine sets of eyes followed me as I walked into the room to find my seat, wearing a dress that was distinctly NOT the Sacred Heart uniform of brown, black, gold, and white plaid. The whole thing was far from my former routine.

The schoolwork also seemed immediately different to me, and not at all like the work kids were doing at West Ridge School in Highland Park, Illinois. It seemed harder and I thought I was screwing up badly. In my mind, I panicked, thinking that maybe I wasn't as smart as I thought I was. And then, reading groups were assigned and I was told to go down to the library with a small group of kids for the accelerated reading group. Again, I was surprised but did my best to hide it so that I wouldn't be noticed.

The school was run by Sister Janet Schmitt and the kids were terrified of her. She had a way about her that said: "Don't f#*k with me, kid. I am NOT in the mood." Youngsters rarely stepped out of line.

While the four younger kids of our family—in 1st, 2nd, 6th, and 7th grade, respectively, at the time of the move—ended up at Sacred Heart, poor Tim and Margie, already in high school, had to start all over. They entered nearby Horlick High School in the 10th and 11th grades at what could possibly be the worst time for a school transfer, depending on the level of introvert versus extrovert.

The upside of entering Racine schools was the fact that we were all a bit of a novelty, a curiosity, to the other kids. There were six of us from "Chicago" and new to Racine. Thank goodness we all possessed a shred of social sensibility and were quickly able to make friends. Growing up in a family of six kids with one shared bathroom meant you'd better be able to get along with others. Even John, who for years got by just fine with an imaginary best friend from the baseball park by the name of "Base," made a new group of friends.

Horlick High was just a few blocks away, past Wadewitz Elementary School, named after a savvy printer who purchased the printing company in Racine that published Little Golden Books. Mr. Wadewitz ran it until the company was bought out by an opportunistic New York investor who likely didn't care about the impact of closing a popular publishing house in some quasi-industrial city in Southeast Wisconsin.

Thus, for the youngest four of us, most of our formative years were defined by the teachers and administrators of Sacred Heart School. The walk to Sacred Heart seemed to always take place in the rain or freezing cold. Winter can be hard. Wisconsin winters haughtily stare down and mock the so-called winters taking place in the rest of the country. School and work move on in the face of wintry conditions most would think unbearable. To Wisconsinites, toughing it through the long winter months is a small source of pride. Wisconsin natives keep their chins up and bear each year of sleet, snow, hail, snow, ice, frigid winds, and a little more snow. They are tougher and stronger because of it and have an NFL team based out of the hinterlands to prove it.

The walk back and forth from Sacred Heart meant each chilly step traced the number of indentations in the sidewalk, and on the ok weather days, there were ants, all sorts of ants. Big, black carpenter ants, medium-sized brown ants and the nasty little red ones that liked to bite if you tried to hold them. They crawled in and around every bit of sidewalk, seemingly oblivious to the big feet stepping by, trying to avoid the cracks so as not to break their mother's backs. The ants—well, we didn't care so much about whether they broke or not.

At some point, the sidewalk path made its way to the church and then to the school and through the mercy of the clerical staff, we were allowed to wait in the foyer on bitter cold days before the school bell rang.

The Greater Milwaukee Archdiocese has historically been known as a more liberal jurisdiction amongst Catholic organizations. We didn't know or appreciate it at the time, but the stretches of the Milwaukee Archdiocese and all its dogma may or may not have something to do with the fact that the head of the organization, Archbishop Rembert Weakland, had been having an affair with a much younger male theologian for decades and was generally more tolerant of certain social positions than others who shared his title.

Every week, the kids at our school helped plan masses and wrote "prayers for the faithful," asking for prayers for anything from the weather, to families, to the injured. Without fail, Archbishop Weakland was included in our prayers, even though not a single one of the kids at Sacred Heart had ever met or seen him. I'm not even sure any of us even knew what an archbishop was, but it had the word "arch" in it, like Superman's arch-enemy Lex Luthor, so he must have been big-time. He was sort of a mythical figure with an odd name that tended to stick with you, and the imagination would go far and wide to try to piece together a picture of this holy figurehead sitting somewhere in a much fancier church in Milwaukee. Not God or Jesus, of course, but important, for sure.

The older grades planning the masses also got to participate in singing, or praying, or some other church task and because it took us out of the classroom, even if just for an hour. This time was our escape. It was meditation meets mindfulness before those terms and practices had names. We put on our coats and sometimes pulled on the boots, hats, mittens, and scarves during snowy winter months. Then we quietly walked down the sidewalk, boys in one line, girls in another, grade by grade across the driveway to the modern-looking, red-carpeted, wooden UFO structure that was our church.

A handful of priests were assigned to our church over the years, from the very old to the very young, but as far as we students were concerned, aside from one priest who was rumored to be an alcoholic, we didn't have anything bad to say about any of them.

Sacred Heart School was not at all one of the "Catholic-lite" type of school that was only Catholic in name, with a religion class that followed a book, and a prayer at the start of the day led by a group of lay teachers. Sacred Heart actually had a few nuns in addition to Sister Janet, our principal.

Sister Janet set the tone for the rest of the school by rarely smiling and if she did, it really didn't fit her face very well, as if the exercise in showing joy to younger kids pained her. Just about every kid in the whole school was scared to death of her, for good reason. Sister Janet managed by fear and had a zero-tolerance policy when it came to kids who failed to toe the line. The school was her everything and she never seemed to take a sick or vacation day. She lived next door to the school in a nice German-looking, two-story brick home with another nun or two. Somehow, you never saw her go in or out of that house and as far as we kids were concerned, she never left the school.

Sister Janet was able to be anywhere and everywhere. She had an air of absolutely no B.S. about her and even the rowdier boys kept themselves dutifully in check when she patrolled the halls. She was exactly what each and every grade school on the planet needed to keep kids precisely in line. If whatever formula she used to maintain order hasn't been recreated for use by other school administrators for all of eternity, it should be.

Sister Janet almost always wore what we all came to think of as the "nun's uniform," which consisted of a set combination of a pressed white blouse, a gray polyester skirt, unbelievably sensible black shoes with support-type-looking hose, and of course, a nun's veil. It gave her extra credibility, which she really didn't need.

Each school year, Sister Janet brought in "Officer Friendly" from the Racine Police Department. He was usually an experienced and kind officer in the force who came in to explain the job of police officers during an all-school presentation. He drove a special "Officer Friendly" police car and talked to us about trusting and not being afraid of the police. Little did he know that any fear we experienced with police officers paled in comparison to our Sacred Heart nuns.

Wrinkled clothing of any kind, whether on her or the kids, was not an option. Our uniforms were made of impossibly stiff synthetic materials that held creases where they were supposed to be, and did not wrinkle.

As long as Sister Janet was anywhere in the school, there was to be no talking in the halls, no pushing, no running, no nothing but a single line from your room to lunch or recess, and that was about it. If a teacher threatened to send you down to the principal's office, you'd better pray for mercy that it didn't actually happen. Because if it did, you were done. Not sure how, but no one knew and no one ever—not ever—wanted to find out.

Sacred Heart also had its share of lay teachers, but few, if any, gave an inch when it came to discipline. Sister Janet strictly ruled the teachers and for the seven years I attended Sacred Heart, only our third-grade teacher, Mrs. Braun, stands out in my memory as being kind. She was very old and slow but soft in her words and actions, like the grandmother every kid imagines. As far as I can recall, third grade was just about the only year that we as students were allowed to collectively exhale and relax, even if just a little bit more than the other years.

Aside from the brief third-grade respite, rules were to be followed and stringently enforced, and that was that, especially with the newest group of what our dad referred to as "shanty Irish" kids from Chicago.

At the beginning of one especially dismal school year, Sister Janet even came up with a way of documenting her displeasure with kids who walked a little too close to the line of disobedience. It was called a "pink slip." Nothing fancy, just a half sheet of paper colored bubble-gum pink with the student's name, date, and a checkmark by any number of infractions ranging from "talking in the hallways" to "fighting" or "cursing." As you might imagine, the latter two were very unlikely to have happened, if ever.

The pink slip had a non-behavioral counterpart known as the "blue slip." You would be handed a blue slip if you managed to forget your homework at home or hadn't bothered to finish it. The blue slip wasn't as bad as the pink slip, but you had to take it home and get it signed by a parent. If the tougher parent was tasked with signing the slip, well, then good luck to you.

The pink and blue slips were a great source of gossip and intrigue amongst the students. "Did you hear about that kid who got a pink slip?" "How many blue slips *DID* she get?" And on and on. The grade-school boys in our family were not strangers to the pink and blue program

Each year during Lent, we were told we had to give something up for the month and a half between Ash Wednesday and Easter. Some of the kids paid attention to this, but for me, I thought sharing just about everything I'd ever had with five older siblings, even when I didn't want to, was "giving up" enough. The nuns, Sister Gladys, Sister Janet, and another two or three teachers whose names I just can't recall, usually gave up sweets. Like *all* sweets. For the entire six weeks. That was simply out of the question from my perspective.

In our family, treats were few and far between and why in the world would I give them up? On the other side of Lent, once Easter passed and without much of a spring break to speak of, each class walked just a half block down the street to Dairy Queen, where we were each treated to a Dilly Bar. Days of such excess were quite rare at Sacred Heart, and we all enjoyed our sugar-induced glee. Spring, Dilly Bars, and summer were just around the corner. The following day, of course, things went back to normal. It was time for the nuns and teachers to get the students right back into line, allowing for but the tiniest glimpses of joy during lunch and recess.

Fortunately, whether by sheer accident or as the Earth's way of self-balancing, the weight of Sister Janet's disciplinarian figure was directly balanced by the existence of a much more permissive counterpart. At Sacred Heart, that was the pastor, Father Mike, the one who blessed our garden and made everything grow like Jack and the Beanstalk. He was young and kind and tall and athletic and played baseball with the kids at recess. Everyone loved him and he would come over and sit with the kids at lunch, eating the same awful lunchroom food off of the same pale-yellow lunch trays—from fish sticks on Fridays, to hamburger-ish hamburgers, to spaghetti, to overcooked and underwhelming rectangles of pizza.

Father Mike's stay at the school seemed much too short, although none of us recall the exact beginning nor end of his tenure.

Whether Father Mike was there or not, the kids all agreed that lunch was the world's best way to break up more than seven hours of intense daily instruction. The lunch menu was placed in the window of the front office every week and rarely, if ever, did the selections bring any degree of excitement. It was the thirty minutes of non-stop chatter that we all loved.

Just before the start of lunch, rows and rows of lunch tables magically appeared after gym class, and were set up single-handedly by the janitor, Mr. Guerra, who had a way of doing more work than every other staff member in the school combined. In the less affluent communities, Catholic schools didn't have the wherewithal or ability to raise funds for excesses like separate gyms, cafeterias, and auditoriums. Catholic schools were built around a "gym-cafetorium" design, where just about every non-classroom event—from sports, to gym to lunch to meetings to plays—were housed in one large area.

Pricier private schools and public schools funded by local taxes always seemed to have much more—a separate gymnasium, a large cafeteria, and in some cases, even an auditorium. Such was not the Catholic school's way. Catholic schools seemed to take it as a point of pride that they barely had enough funding to keep the kids and parents above the imaginary line where complaints start to register.

As for Mr. Guerra, we were taught to address him with a proper amount of respect and greeted him each time he passed us by in the hallway, which was always met without any words, just a simple nod of the head. He had one of those all-knowing demeanors that made you instantly aware of the fact that your background and experience would either never be as interesting or terrible as his.

Mr. Guerra moved slowly and deliberately, pushing a trash can on wheels or a cart, and looked at you without even opening his mouth, yet communicating very clearly, as if to say: "Hello, good day, and I forgive you for having to clean up your puke all over the hallway floor. I know you were embarrassed and so I didn't tell anyone." He never spoke to any of us or addressed us, but quietly and meticulously covered every corner of the school with old-school antibacterial cleaners like bleach and other stuff that was as strong as lye, floor wax, and window cleaner.

Each classroom contained about twenty-five kids. Eight years is a really long time to spend with the same group of young people. You find yourself weaving in and out of different friendships and alliances for the sheer sake of keeping it interesting. Remarkably, there were very different people to hang out with back at Sacred Heart School. Sometimes, you'd get lucky and there would be a transfer kid bringing in fresh, new air to our stale class, like my friend Kelly.

We all immediately knew Kelly was different. She was tough and athletic and pretty and didn't give a damn about the management-by-fear going on at Sacred Heart. She was a rock star in her own right, and I was instantly in awe of her. She had qualities that set her apart from the other kids and made her popular as a result, but most of all, she took absolutely zero shit from anyone.

Kelly was the second youngest of a family of nine kids, with parents who ran a tavern on the west side of town. Consistent with the "why not?" parenting approach many parents tend to follow with the youngest child, for some reason, I was allowed to go hang out at their family tavern on a fairly regular basis. Kelly, her younger sister, Maureen, and I would play basketball in the parking lot of the bar with the

49

neighborhood kids. It was located in a gritty side of town, but the family ran a respectable business with good food and so people didn't bother them.

I was a crappy athlete, but just hanging around Kelly and her sisters and trying to play basketball made me a little better. And we played ball with the scrappy neighborhood girls. The same ones who, when you asked them where they lived, looked you straight in the eye in a nonchalant way and responded in a very matter-of-fact way, announcing they lived in "N-ville." Except they didn't say N-ville. They said the real N-word. The one we would never have dared to say in our family or at school. It just wasn't allowed. We all knew as far back as we could remember that it was wrong. Yet, the term rolled off the tongues of the people who lived there as easily as a "Hi!" or a "Nice to meet you..." or "Do you know what time it is?" sort of conversation.

Many put this reference, which is no doubt shocking and upsetting, out of their minds for years and years. That is, until one day there were discussions about race relations in Racine. The memory of the term popped up out of nowhere like a bad penny, making both the brain and the heart hurt to realize that it was ever a word to come to life to only evolve into a source of hatred and cruelty.

How and why that area of town came to be called that was an absolute mystery. Over time, outsiders never having set foot in Racine or any of the Racine Unified School District schools would use this sort of thing as a basis to judge Racine, its people, and its institutions. Some would accuse its inhabitants of systemic racism against the African American community. Maybe they were right, maybe they were wrong, but coming from an outside world of privilege and opportunities never known to the vast majority of those they claimed to care about while doing nothing to try to change things for the better. Regardless, that was what that part of town was called. Nor were its younger residents the sort of girls and boys who had a lot of patience with stupid questions, so I never asked.

That Nun is not Very Nice

IN SCHOOL, KELLY WAS FEARLESS. She was growing up in a huge family with a bar next door in a tough neighborhood. And oddly, even with Sister Janet at the helm, there was no shortage of excitement at Sacred Heart. You'd think it would be an oppressive place, but kids with average home situations found school to be an escape. The bad teachers must have known they were bad and wouldn't go crying to Sister Janet for help. Even if they were decent teachers, it meant a wee bit of failure and in the top nun's eyes, this was not an option in the halls of Sacred Heart School.

One day in fifth grade, a day that started like many of the other hundreds of cold, wet, and gray indecipherably winter-into-spring types of day, Kelly decided she'd had enough with Sister Gladys. By then, we were all at our breaking point, but were too afraid to do anything about it. Sister Gladys was too harsh, too mean-spirited, too angry.

Once, one of our classmates, Danny, legitimately took a serious header onto the ice-covered concrete coming off of a gargantuan snow pile at the end of our church parking lot turned playground. He threw up in the hallway, which was followed by one of Mr. Guerra the janitor's religious applications of an orangey sawdust mixture with an indescribably bad smell. Danny came back to the classroom and was "falling asleep" at his desk. Clearly this was well ahead of concussion-protocol days, but nevertheless, Sister Gladys handled the situation with aplomb, accusing Danny of "faking it," impatiently lashed out at him, and telling him to sit up properly in his chair.

As much as I tried to fly under Sister Gladys's piercing dark eyes and accompanying radar, I must have annoyed her one day without even trying, which was the disappointing part. At least then I would have scored some minor personal fulfillment points. A group of girls, including me, was standing by the back of the classroom without any boys around, when she verbally pounced on what was my very prepubescent self, telling me—rather shouting at me—in a very unceremonious announcement: "You need a bra!"

No warning, no mincing words, no whispering. That was it. Approach life with chainsaw communications. That was her mantra. Inside, my soul shrank a little bit that day. As if I didn't have enough to be embarrassed about, she piled on shame with reckless abandon. I swallowed a great big bunch of tears and let them out later when I was at home, alone.

And so it was not long after, on what seemed like another endless school day, that Kelly walked out of Sister Gladys's class about half way through. It went something like this.

Sister Gladys told Kelly, "Now you sit down!"

And Kelly, who was probably going to sharpen a pencil or throw out some trash and was not at all afraid of or a stranger to conflict, walked out, telling Sister Gladys, "You're such a bitch."

And she walked her ass right out of the classroom like a boss. She was entirely right. Sister Gladys was a bitch and God help me, even though she was doing "God's work" in her chosen vocation, she was miserable and mean and had a face that was too frozen from frowning in constant disapproval of just about every damn thing around her to crack a decent smile.

The entire class, including Sister Gladys, sat there, mouths agape, wondering what the hell had just happened. There was the initial shockwave that reverberated through each line of desks. Then, some of us must have been thinking, "Kelly's 100 percent right on that," but never, ever, ever would have had half a nerve to get to the point where we'd actually vocalize the thought.

Ultimately, most of us didn't even remember Kelly coming back that day. Had she walked home? Was she intercepted by

Sister Janet in the hallway and beaten to a pulp? We were afraid and excited and although it was one of the high points of my grade-school career, it really had nothing to do with me. I honestly have no clue how things went down after that other than an eerily silent couple of hours before we went home. As far as I know, no one said a thing to their parents. We were still in a state of disbelief and repeating the story might have led to unknown repercussions.

The next day, Kelly returned to class as though nothing had happened. And despite the fact that she would be loath to admit it and furious that any of us could sense it, Sister Gladys was taken down a notch from that point on. At least from the perspective of our classroom, she was oddly on better behavior. This made most of us incredibly concerned about when the other shoe would drop, but somehow, it never did. She even smiled a few times, maybe. It was psychological warfare and she was winning, again.

Sports Fails

YEAR AFTER YEAR, THE CATHOLIC grade school program was the same. Class, recess, lunch, Christmas break that never lasted nearly long enough, Lent, Dairy Queen Dilly Bars at the end of Lent, and Mass once a week. School meant academics and an opportunity for socializing. The academic part of school provided a sense of order and certainty and I was actually good at it.

To me, being among the smarter kids in the class, helped balance out the repeated humiliation I experienced in being really bad at just about every athletic endeavor I tried. Not that anyone cared, but kids tend to think that everyone cares about everything. They usually don't. At least not as much little-kid brains tend to believe. So with my imaginary belief that it actually mattered to others how bad I was in sports, I tried much harder to succeed at academics. Again, it was a matter of balance.

Watching sports—not playing—was more of a thing in our family. A huge television the size of an armoire sat on the floor in our living room. It was accompanied by a remote-control clicker the size of a toaster oven. The clicker didn't work very well, which meant the younger kids were recruited to change the channels. In a way, we kids were the *de facto* remote controls. Since we were lower in the pecking order on the seating arrangement, we were kicked off the couch and relegated to watching television while seated cross-legged on the scratchy, gray-wool-carpeted floor. Getting up every few minutes to change the channel didn't really make our state much worse and so we barely noticed that we were asked to "change the channel." Those words became more ambient noise to us and we complied without even knowing it.

The whole family loved the Cubs and the Bears and watching whatever non-Wisconsin team we could find on WGN out of Chicago on our old bunny-ear-antenna television, because it was free. We rarely went to live sporting events.

Playing sports of any kind was entirely up to us. There was no expectation that working parents would get you to and from practice or that they would have time to make it to your games. Back then, seeing parents at kids' sporting events was more of an exception than the norm.

Personally, I was so bad at sports that this played a role later in life when it came to my decision-making process in choosing a spouse. I married a guy ridiculously competitive and gifted at any sport he cared to try. It would give our children at least half a fighting chance. Again, balance.

For me, whether track or softball or cheerleading, my efforts and corresponding outcomes were equally sub-par. The pinnacle of my lackluster approach to athletic activities happened over the summer between 6th and 7th grade, when one of the more competitive dads decided he would coach us. What made it even worse was the fact that no assistant coach was there to talk some sense into him when he went off the deep end of obsessively trying to win.

He was one of those dads who even the kids knew had either been an awful athlete himself or needed a winning team to give his unremarkable image a boost in the eyes of the other dads. So I, one of the least effective members of the team, if not *the* most ineffective team member, was placed in the right-field position. With the majority of batters being right-handed, it was rare to get a hit over to right field.

Our master-strategist softball coach put me in that position so I would face the fewest amount of hits that ended up coming my way. To make absolutely certain I had next to no contact with the ball, our coach came up with the additional strategy that I would switch spots with the much more athletic left fielder any time a left-handed hitter stepped up to the plate. He'd stop the game in front of everyone—the players, the other team, and the parents—raise his hands, and motion for me to get over to left field so that I wouldn't screw things up. Sometimes, we would get an opponent on the other team who would step up to the plate, pretending to be a left-handed hitter, and we would start running to the opposite fields to switch, only to realize she was messing with us when she went back to her right-handed stance.

The fun continued in junior high track and field. Sports were "no-cut," meaning that anyone could join the team, leaving coaches with a bit of a quandary. What to do with the average to below-average athletes in track? I mean, you have to put them somewhere. In my case, that meant one of the throwing or jumping type events. Without speed or endurance or a care in the world about winning, for that matter, young "athletes" like me who couldn't be completely benched or shelved in track found themselves in the exciting event of the shotput, or the long jump, or if you were super-lucky, the high jump. But track meets are long. Really long. Like all day in crappy spring weather on Lake Michigan in Southeast Wisconsin long. Our coach, who was in his 30s or 60s—no one could really tell—was single and had no kids himself.

It must have been an incredible disappointment to him to have such underperformers like me on his team. Many of us were there solely because we didn't have anything better to do, and after all, it was free. And though it was clear I was not alone with a small group of lower-echelon track and field teammates, I knew very well that the coach either didn't care if I was there, or didn't want me there at all. So with the small remaining amount of self-respect I managed to keep after years of colossal sports failures, I quit mid-season. I didn't consult anyone. I doubt I even had a conversation. I just quit. You're welcome, Coach Marty.

If I were to win anything at all, it had to be in the classroom, where I only had one serious competitor: Aaron Goodman. He was super-smart and as serious and about as well-behaved as the teacher. He even looked the part of the smart kid—thick classes, buzz cut and an austere demeanor you didn't typically find in grade-school students. It was as though he was more advanced than the rest of us both intellectually and emotionally. To me, it seemed that he couldn't wait to get the school thing over with and start teaching and making money himself.

Our own teachers were merciless, pitting us one against one, student versus student, in nonstop games of "around the world" math competitions and routine spelling bees. Sometimes, Aaron would beat me, and whether he won or lost, he was so gracious and kind about it that I actually found it irritating.

The one tiny corner of the academic universe that I called my own were the standardized tests. They presented the singular opportunity I had to save face in front of my peers, after repeated humiliations at every possible level in competitive sports. That is, of course, assuming anyone cared—and they probably didn't. I was in the minority by far, because I absolutely loved the whole standardized test process. Instead of the regular class schedule, we would be given a folder with math and reading questions and a sheet to carefully fill in tiny little circles with multiple-choice answers in pencil.

Once finished with the first folder, students would quietly walk to the teacher's desk and replace the test in the box with the next folder and set of questions. To me, academics were the only sort of competition I was actually ever good at and so I made it my own competition of madly getting through the questions so that I'd be able to march up in front of my classmates and show them how smart I was by finishing way ahead of them. Or so I let myself believe.

The teachers may have been viewed as cruel and heartless dictators. But at least they were teaching us something. The coaches, well, they were entirely different animals. They weren't winning for the kids; they were winning for themselves and unknowingly setting the stage for a complete reversal in the way future grade-school and middle-school sports and coaching would look. In the future, things were not always driven by the best or the smartest coaches, but rather by parents seeking revenge on their childhood coaches, which never bodes well.

After decades of separation from Catholic grade-school life, most of us came to understand and empathize with the tougher school administrators long after leaving Sacred Heart. They weren't necessarily mean or misanthropic *per se*; they were just afraid of losing control to a bunch of kids. That would have meant defeat and humiliation. No one wants that. When we were young, all they had to do was threaten us with something that might reach our parents. To us, they were great big, scary, bullies like the tall trees in a dark and mysterious forest. As we grew up, they were exposed like bare trees showing their frail branches in the middle of winter.

The Smoke and the Smokers

WISCONSIN WAS IN MANY WAYS like an anti-California. By and large, there was nothing "granola" about the nature of the people who lived in the Badger State. Back then, it wasn't a place where people did yoga or acupuncture or ate organic foods or tried to get more yogurt or greens into their diets. If it didn't taste good, why bother?

People tended to eat what they wanted, drink what they wanted, and smoke what they wanted. Farmers, blue-collar workers, and rural people took a very simple approach to life and really didn't worry about their way of life, or what others may have thought about it. Overall, the approach led to less stress, but the upshot was a fairly shoddy physical frame with complimenting health issues by the time you reached 40.

When I was little, cigarette smokers seemed to be everywhere. Our mom smoked an absurd number of cigarettes throughout the day. She didn't drink at all, and very understandably, needed some sort of release from the chaos of six kids and pets that seem to appear and multiply in spades. Instead, cigarettes were her release. She'd get close to finishing one cigarette and compulsively light up another one almost immediately. To many smokers, cigarette smoke becomes an oxygen that is inhaled like ambient air.

Usually, one of us would be sent down to Open Pantry to buy packs of L&M cigarettes for her. It didn't matter if there was a finder's fee or not; most of us went willingly because it was something to do. You also would not want to mess with someone's constitutional right to smoke cigarettes throughout the day. Later, the cigarette of choice, L&Ms, morphed into Marlboro Reds—the box, not the soft packs, because they kept up better in a purse filled with a bunch of stuff she may or may not have needed throughout the day or for any particular type of outing.

You might think it would raise an eyebrow or two when an eight- or ten-year-old kid showed up at the convenience store or gas station counter asking for a very specific pack of cigarettes. Not at all. Back then, we never had to carry a note from Mom saying it was ok for us to buy cigarettes. No questions were asked about our age when we presented a few crumpled dollar bills. The exchange happened even when the kid on the other side of the counter was quite clearly below double digits. No one gave a care in the world about whether a little girl or boy with a semi-toothless smile asked to buy a pack of cigarettes for Mom. We would walk down or take our bikes to the store because it gave us a sense of purpose, a goal, something to do.

Open Pantry became an odd gathering place for neighborhood kids without enough to do in the summer. In a way, it was a "pre-bar" for a lot of us, and it broke up the long, monotonous dog days of June, July, and August. No electronic devices, no phones, not a lot of anything really, with the exception of a prehistoric black-and-white video game called *Pong* that tried its best to mimic ping-pong on a TV screen. In truth, the video version "pong" was much slower than ping-pong in real life, and involved hardly any skill.

Later, we did score an Atari game system, which distracted us for a while, but the gamers took too long to create new games and couldn't keep up with the interest of the kids playing them. Joysticks were too basic and could only keep your attention for so long. There were no decent cartoons during the week either. That isn't necessarily a complaint, but serves to emphasize just how important Saturday morning cartoons really were for kids in the 1970s and early 80s. For a kid like me, who was aggressively average at sports, but really good at getting through homework quickly, errands were a distraction, even if it did mean buying cigarettes, which I absolutely despised. So I'd go out, and would try to hustle a candy bar or treat of some kind in exchange. Marathons—the long, skinny, braided, chocolate-covered caramel candy bars—went for 25 cents. Candy nirvana. Kids are like addicts when it comes to candy. They will do whatever it takes to get it, hoard it, eat it and get some more.

Cigarettes were a commodity traded and bartered in our home, much like in prison. How they kept popping up everywhere and any-where was a mystery. They never ran out. Ever. Yet, there just wasn't a lot of extra cash on hand. There had to be a hustle. Everyone 16 or older smoked; eventually, our mom started hiding her cigarettes. The kids in the family would other-wise swipe them ruthlessly from their siblings.

Eventually, my siblings realized they'd need money to buy cigarettes and freedom and so they worked different jobs to keep an open stream of access to the things they wanted most: cigarettes. And if the older kids in the family somehow thought I wasn't 100 percent serious when I yelled, "I'll tell!" at them when I caught them doing something they weren't supposed to do, well, I suppose, here it is.

This practice of working for cigarettes did not apply to the two youngest kids, Morgan and me, because we hadn't quite reached our full smoking potential yet. But Morgan and I did at least come to acknowledge how important the smoking habit was to every other member of our family. One Christmas, after collecting money from doing little chores, I used the five dollars in coins and bills I'd saved to buy a present for my brother John. Why him versus any other sibling remains a mystery.

I marched myself and my five bucks to the gas station and bought him a full carton of Marlboro Reds. I didn't wrap the carton of cigarettes. I presented it to him on Christmas morning, high in the air, like a trophy. The bright red and black writing on the carton may even have glowed.

I kept the surprise to myself and the entire family beamed with pride when they realized the results of my industrious side. That single carton, a total of 200 cigarettes, may have been one of the most thoughtful, memorable, and appreciated gifts I've ever given to any of my siblings. That moment was the most positive attention I received all year.

Cigarettes would be ok if they could just figure out a way of keeping to themselves. And not causing cancer or emphysema. But cigarettes are smelly and messy and if you're a kid and you're not careful, they will find a way of singeing your hair or clothes if you get too close. It's always the kid's fault for not being careful, mind you.

Cigarettes find a way to creep into the personal space of everyone around the smoker. Ashes and cigarette butts had a way of showing up in just about every part of our lives. If we searched our mom's purse for gum or candy, any remaining products would usually be so studded with pieces of tobacco, like tiny porcu-pines, that no person in their right mind would want them, not even Sam the Great Dane.

In the Pinto or used station wagon, a drive with my mom usually meant sitting surrounded by overwhelming clouds of thick white smoke. Most times, I'd cover my mouth and breathe through my shirt, imagining this obvious protest would clearly get her to rethink her smoking habit, but of course, it never did. She clearly needed something for the endless supply of stressors in her life. Nicotine fit the bill and the addictive part of it was not a joke. So when I protested her habit, in whatever subtle or direct way I imagined, either she pretended to ignore me or didn't notice at all, but she smoked and smoked away.

The house had an abundance of various old ashtrays; some were purchased, some were found, and some were even lovingly made by school-age children during art class, under the close supervision of their smoker art teachers. It was usually one kid's job to be in charge of emptying out the ashtrays.

Mom: "Hey! It's your turn to empty the ashtrays!!"

Child: "Why do I have to empty them?"

Mom: "Because I asked you to, and it's your job!"

Child: (Silently wondering what in the world it took to make it "his/her" job, anyway).

Mom: "Hey! Empty the ashtrays!"

Over and over. Again and again.

Such a discussion usually meant that a small battle of wills came about and the one who hated the residue of ashes or tar on anything, would be the one doing the emptying. And somehow it usually involved a much larger mess trying to deftly transfer several days of ashes and cigarette butts to the garbage.

I was typically the weakest link, ready to give up before the rest of the holdouts. I also had a visceral reaction of sorts whenever our mom yelled. She had a loud, deep, powerful voice and at full bore, it cut into my soul like a machete. She didn't need to hit anyone; her voice was her greatest weapon and she used it like a boss.

If you were with her out in public—a store, the mall, or even a library—and you wandered out of sight, you'd better believe you'd hear her shouting your name from 100 yards away. That bellow was powerful enough to stop you dead in your tracks and bring you running back, no questions asked.

On the other hand, our dad had the type of voice that sounded as though he was always just on the verge of breaking out in song or laughter, which meant that the lion's share of discipline unfairly landed in our mom's lap. Hence, the cigarettes.

At one point, out of frustration or boredom, Morgan stole a pack of Kent cigarettes from Mom's purse. The two of us tried smoking them. We wanted to look like big kids, and we wanted to be like Mom, even if we hated the habit. At the time, we were about seven or eight years old, and had no clue about the dangers, except maybe the lighting matches and causing fires part. We managed to light ourselves two cigarettes and had the gumption (you can imagine, there are more appropriate, less appropriate descriptive terms I won't use…) to walk down the sidewalk, smoking for all to see.

By some miracle, not a single parent or kid saw us. We got bored and decided to put them out. We also realized the smoking wasn't all it was cracked up to be, especially when you weren't inhaling. Eventually, every single one of my older siblings took up smoking to one degree or another; some stayed loyal to the cause while others walked away from it. To their credit, it could not have been easy when others continued to smoke around you in a smoker-y culture.

Not long after the great cigarette heist, Morgan stole Mom's keys to the family station wagon and the two of us went out to the driveway to give it a spin. At least a week or two separated the stolen cigarette ordeal and the station wagon event, which would more fairly be described as a disaster.

Even as kids, we came to appreciate and respect a "cooling down" period from what had to be a couple of irate parents. Morgan got behind the wheel and I excitedly jumped in the front passenger seat. He managed to reach his foot far enough down to press on the accelerator, started the ignition, and away we went, into a good-sized fence, completely knocking it down.

Whether he hit the brakes or not would be pretty important information, but somehow and through some sort of divine intervention, the station wagon came to a stop before careening off into the nearby garage and we escaped unscathed, at least physically. We were good kids doing stupid things on a fairly regular basis. The constant smoking. No wonder.

I regularly staged various forms of protest to our mom's smoking, from holding my nose, to pulling my shirt up over my face, to opening every possible window in our house. Of course, it didn't help to actually verbalize anything about my distaste, so I thought the clever approach of just being annoying about her smoking would do the trick. But it didn't.

Nevertheless, in fifth grade, in an effort to elevate what had become a concerted anti-smoking protest, I decided that I would do a science fair project on the dangers of smoking, with an explanation of the awful symptoms and results of lung cancer.

My friend Mary was my science fair partner and her mom was a nurse. We therefore scored on the project materials. Mary somehow managed to get us these teeny-tiny transparent model lungs made of foam and plastic from the American Lung Association or some other equally anti-smoking group for our project. We were sure we would win that science fair. The transparent covering on the lungs let viewers see straight into the fake lungs, which turned tar-colored when you attached a lit cigarette, squeezed the lung, and allowed the smoke to be drawn in.

I was so confident. I really thought ours was a shoe-in. It was medical and complicated and dripping with science, after all. And none of those other kids even approached the level of sophistication we had. Carcinogens. Mechanism of injury, models, scientific controls, a hypothesis—the whole bit. We worked so hard and couldn't wait until the winners were announced.

But Mary and I didn't even place in the top three. Too many smokers—everywhere. Not just at home, but at school too, it turned out. And in retrospect, I am fairly certain that none of the smokers wanted to hear about the dangers of smoking from a couple of little kids who thought they knew it all.

Year upon year, I was losing my ill-conceived personal battle against the smokers. It was in the house, in restaurants, and all around. Smoking in the car was another thing. The car became a smoking prison. No escape. The ashtray in the car was never cleaned. In fact, maybe not ever. There was some sort of godless miracle of the loaves going on. The light-brown cigarette butts colored with shimmery, light-pink Revlon lipstick reached the very top of the tray, just barely staying within the container. If our mom braked too quickly, ashes and cigarette butts fell to the floor with some ashes floating through the air like dandelions in the summer.

Although our mom did stop smoking many, many years afterwards as far as we knew, it took a heart attack forty years later and a very convincing, zero-tolerance cardiologist lacking any sense of humor to get her to kick an addiction that held a power over her more than anything or anyone else. She had already been diagnosed with asthma, COPD, and emphysema. The fact that cigarettes were incredibly addicting was already well-known and established in the literature and in our experience, it had a grip on her and would not let go.

Cigarette smoking was one thing. Back then, smoking was accepted because it was everywhere and the majority of the population seemed to smoke at some point or another. After all, the Surgeon General may have warned against smoking, but he didn't ban it, which meant, of course, he allowed it. Some of the members of my family, however, decided it was within their reach to take the world of smoking up a notch and parlayed their cigarette-smoking experience into marijuana.

Once again, the kids in our family were a bit too ahead of their time in an accidental, unacceptable, and illegal kind of way. Their experiences with weed would not have been heralded as a "trailblazer" type of thing. Marijuana was a controlled substance, after all, and there was the technical issue of breaking the law and putting yourself at the mercy of the Racine Police Department if you got busted. Without any decent contacts at the police department and no lawyer friends to speak of, it was user beware.

Truth be told, marijuana was perfectly fine and was even prescribed by doctors for decades until the Prohibition, when it was outlawed, along with alcohol. For reasons unknown, possibly due to more powerful alcohol lobbyists, booze carried the day when Prohibition was repealed with the Twenty-First Amendment. Marijuana was kicked to the curb, remained off limits, and was classified as the type of substance no law-abiding member of the good old boys' club would ever be caught using.

Buying weed might have been out of reach for most Wisconsin teens, but growing it was another matter altogether. It was more of a technicality, like the Surgeon General warning on a pack of cigarettes. If you're just growing some nice plants that give you the added benefit of a high, well, why not?

It just so happened that our mom had a host of soft skills. One of them was gardening, although this was another one of those skill-transfers with unintended results. She watered and weeded and planted whenever she had a spare moment, and it was a relatively easy matter for the boys to translate what they witnessed of her agricultural efforts into an at-home weed-growing enterprise. Doing so was just another thing in a long line of missed opportunities when it came to my siblings. They were not just a few years—but decades—ahead of growing legal cannabis in the states.

On a few occasions, our mom found suspicious-looking new plants growing in the yard next to perennials like tiger lilies or violets or rhubarb. These tiny new sprouts didn't last long, though, since she treated them like an invasive species and weeded them out.

Frustrated by a few failed attempts at growing an outdoor crop, our brother John, who honestly had a more creative approach to most things, decided to take his growing operation inside. He found a secret place, learned how to grow marijuana from seed, to seedling, to full-blown, ready-to-harvest stuff, within the confines of a crawl space conveniently located at the back of his closet. Our parents never knew. But I did and when no one was around, I'd scoot back to the end of the closet, open the crawl space door, and check on the progress of seedlings under the bright purple ultra-violet lights on a daily basis. It was like overseeing the keeping of a meticulously farmed, delicate, urban garden. I found it exciting. No one knew that I knew and for that, I felt I had a pretty fair advantage for future bargaining my way out of trouble, if I ever needed it.

Remarkably, every once in a while, in what was surely the ultimate leap of faith, our parents went away for a few days. My brothers, opportunists that they were, usually took these a very small windows of time to have everyone they knew over for a party.

We had a code in our family that no one dared break; you never told on a sibling. If you did, that sibling surely had something much worse on you and if that sibling didn't, you'd better prepare yourself for a serious ass-kicking. Even the greatest weapon in my revenge arsenal—the ability to disclose the crawl space grow to our parents—never came to see the light of day. I was too afraid. Plus, not a single one of us wanted to hear the yelling and arguing that followed any "bad news" or "bad actions" by a co-conspirator sibling.

Sometimes, though, one of us would do something so bad or so obviously above the radar that no code could save us from discovery by our parents. Here's an example.

One of the teenagers drove our nice, new, red Ford sedan—given to our mom by her elderly, disabled father who could no longer drive due to a series of strokes—into a building. It wasn't so much the crashing that enraged Mom. It was the drinking plus driving plus trying to reach under the steering column for a dropped, lit cigarette that really pissed her off.

Our parents and the unnamed teenage sibling came home from the ER late that night, stitches to the teenager's chin and all. It had all come down to one little cigarette. It could have gone out, maybe it didn't roll too forward on the floor mats, or maybe it wasn't dropped at all. And the entire trajectory of the story would have changed, or maybe there would be no story at all.

Instead, our sibling came home with irate parents and the whole house woke up while our parents yelled and yelled and yelled. It was moments like that which scared all of us. We were afraid that the already delicate balance in our parents' marriage was teetering closer to a break.

Kids always think it's their fault. It's not. It never is.

It was our "no-tell" code, though, that largely led John to decide he would speed up his crawl-space harvest and smoke freely with his friends in the house while the parents were gone. We had no internet and although we did have an impressive *Encyclopedia Britannica* set from a garage sale find, it was very unlikely to have a unit dedicated to the harvest of Wisconsin-grown marijuana plants. Which led to the use of instinct. When it comes to teenage boys, instinct and decision-making tend to be a pretty bad combination, leading to even worse decisions.

The harvest went something like this. John and his band of fellow marijuana aficionados took everything they could gather from the crawl space, put it on a couple of old cookie sheets, and stuck it in the oven for a "quick dry" they probably hoped would end up with a good-quality product to share while the parents were out of town.

Morgan and I saw it all, sneaking around like ninjas, making ourselves invisible because we knew we'd be the ones in a lot of trouble if we got caught. The problem with putting a bunch of fresh, green weed in the oven is that it creates the nastiest, skunkiest smell you could ever imagine. Worse than the "walking down the street past a guy smoking weed" smell. It was combined with some sort of vapor from the drying plants and it lingered in the air for days. Our parents came home to smell some remnants, even after best efforts to open every single window and door in the middle of winter. How the older kids talked their way out of that incident will never be known. Other than the weather, maybe things were a little West Coast after all in our house.

But another time, after a blow-out party a few years later, our parents came back early and found a bunch of hungover kids lying around our living room floor. Another event for the ages. The yelling was off the charts and without a solid defense of any kind, John had no real excuse or response. So, they kicked him out. A high-school kid. They kicked him out.

I have no idea where he went or for how long but hearing your parents kick your brother out on the street is pretty damned jarring. Eventually, he came back and not another word was said, and not another party of the sort of magnitude was ever attempted at 2932 North-western Avenue in Racine, Wisconsin.

Neighborhood of Immigrant Dreams

Our homestead stood out from most of the houses on the block. For starters, the building took up a quarter of the block or so. It was a bit of a showoff. The other half of the block was a series of homes of various shapes and sizes, with smaller, more manageable families. The size of the house and the yard allowed for some much-needed privacy for a family with a lot of kids, large dogs, and chaos. You just can't live too close to other neighbors when there was always something going down—a dog barking, kids fighting, and some variety of trouble brewing several times a day.

Our house also happened to be on a sort of busy corner; just across from Hanson's Funeral Home. Hanson's was a beautiful, old, colonial-style building with a great big yard. Beautiful.

Nevertheless, it was a funeral home that had been passed down generation to generation by a group of Swedish immigrants. As little kids, we were convinced something nefarious had to be going on. Nefarious, as beyond the typical dead people in a funeral home sort of thing because kids thrive on mystery and danger and the sort of scary things you see on TV.

As much as we tried to peek through the windows, we never got up the nerve to get close enough. We lived in the comfort of the great big yard buffering us from the actual place of dead bodies. And then one day, my older sister Margie swore she saw something in the attic window:

"They're cutting up bodies at Hanson's!!!"

Our mom, oddly cool about the whole thing, responded calmly: "No, they're not. What are you talking about??"

"They are. They're cutting them. I saw them! Up in the attic window!"

Margie wasn't exactly scared, just convinced. And probably more irritated that her own mother didn't believe her.

This meant the younger kids in the family were petrified, although time went by and we forgot about it. Until the time my sister went out on a date with one of the late-teenage sons of the funeral director. She must have come up with a way to ask about it.

The response?

"Oh, yeah. You see, I have this hobby where I work with mannequins."

And to most people, the entire exchange and conversation would have ended there. Whether in disbelief or disconnect, the discussion should end. Because anyone else would have headed for the hills. Not Margie.

Her response?

A good question. A reasonable question. But I don't think she had one. What do you say to that? You would think he would have come up with something a little better. Maybe he did have a "mannequin hobby." But by then, we'd all decided it would have been much better if he'd just admitted to cutting bodies up for no good reason, because at least that seemed realistic. But a mannequin thing? We were dubious.

That was my sister's first and last date with the guy. The fact that there even was a first date in the first place mystified us all.

Most of our neighbors were hard-working, blue-collar families living mostly in second-generation, ranch-style homes. They were members of the newer immigrant wave, largely from Eastern Europe, fleeing countries with wildly unpredictable rulers. They came from Serbia, Romania, Armenia, Yugoslavia, Greece, and other places, seeking their version of the American dream. The parents found work and were able to afford their own piece of the earth in the land of the free. In the grand scheme of the American Way, each and every one of these families fit in. But when compared to the late-generation Wisconsinites, the newest arrivals had less, were a bit marginalized, and didn't ask or expect much from the American Dream they hoped to at least come to understand. To be here was enough.

Our neighborhood was filled with accents, lots of accents. The parents of most of the kids who lived on our street were just learning English. Some of the more introverted moms barely spoke to you at all. They either didn't want to fumble through a trivial conversation with an American kid, or they didn't care.

It helped that our dad found a way to befriend just about anyone he came across. He got to know an Armenian guy named Larry who owned a service station down the street. Our dad likely walked in to pay for gas, met Larry, and took it from there. Larry had a nice wife and family but shared the same wandering eye as our dad. Whether that similarity brought them together, emboldened them in their own philandering ways, or had absolutely nothing to do with their friendship, I'll never know.

Larry kept a massive, scary-looking Rott-weiler down at the gas station to protect the property. The dog wore a large metal choke collar and sat next to the building, looking to hurt intruders. On weekends and after school, I'd walk a mile down Northwestern Avenue, past Sacred Heart School and Church, past the

Dairy Queen, and on to Larry's service station to walk that dog. By myself. Wherever I wanted. He protected me like a hired guard and if I could have, I would have brought him home and kept him forever.

* * *

Every summer, Racine was the host to a range of festivals started by homesick immigrants wanting to feel a bit of home while showcasing the best of their respective cultural heritages. To some, it became a bit of a competition between the cultural groups. There was a Greek Fest, Serbian Fest, Festa Italiana, Armenian Fest, and more. Each had its own variety of music blaring out of large speakers. There was lots of dancing in ethnic costumes, with foods that were culturally similar and yet different.

Each year on June 19th, Racine's west side hosted the "Juneteenth Celebration" to acknowledge the history of ending slavery in the United States and to celebrate the African American community. It was a huge, loud, all-out party. When you drove by, you immediately knew this was the best of the fests. The weather was usually hot and sunny and the festivities were held in a city park by the lakefront with a massive field of green grass bordered by tall oak and maple trees with industrial-sized barbeque grills flaming. Everyone laughed and played and ate all day long, as if disagreements and race relations were figments of the imagination.

From an outsider's perspective, the various festivals were populated by the very members of the celebrated cultural group, with maybe five to ten percent from the public. These were more like large-scale parties or barbeques organized by a corresponding cultural group; if they made a little extra money while they were at it, even better.

I tried so hard to befriend the first-generation kids in our neighborhood and wanted them to come over to our house to play in the worst way. Only a few kids from my school lived within walking distance; the others took the bus and there seemed to be absolutely no rhyme nor reason to the process in terms of the families from neighborhoods all over town who decided to send their kids to Sacred Heart School. I extended invitation after invitation after invitation for other kids to come play, in the yard, in the house, in the lot next to our home, whether to neighborhood classmates from school or even just neighbor kids who went to the local public school. The answer was invariably a non-negotiable: "No. I can't."

I never pressed any of the kids on the "Why not?" but over time, I came to realize that it might have had something to do with my four quasi-criminal older brothers. Not criminal in the sense that they ever did anything that directly hurt anyone. They just didn't like rules all that much and were bored, like most of their friends who never got into organized sports. Add to that the likelihood that at some point, word must have spread about the fort in the backyard where kids smoked pot, or the pot growing in the yard, or the pot growing inside the home in a crawlspace.

Decades later, such activities would have been praised as entrepreneurial or forward-thinking. Not then, though. Our neighbors were blue-collar and simple and strict with their kids and were especially careful about working squarely within a set of rules and laws set out by state and local police. They wanted to stay here and putting their children in an environment like ours was out of the question. In a way, even at the time, I couldn't really blame them. Even though no abuse or trauma or newsworthy events occurred for the most part, it just wasn't worth risking sending their daughters into our semi-lawless environment.

All Those Kids

PEOPLE WHO COME FROM SMALL families might think that having a lot of kids leads to a disproportionate level of care as each kid comes into the family. They're right. It's simply a numbers versus coverage thing. It's not that our parents kept having kids with the thought that the younger kids wouldn't get the same amount of attention. I think they just liked having a lot of offspring and assumed it would all continue to work itself out somehow.

Growing up with five siblings in an Irish family, a couple of dogs, a couple of cats, as well as some miscellaneous feathered or scaled pets, was nothing short of chaotic. In some ways, things did work themselves out. Each and every one of us became incredibly self-sufficient adults—if we wanted to be self-sufficient, that is. At the time, though, the general approach was that maybe the older kids would help the younger ones out, or maybe not. Once the older kids grew up, there might be more time for the younger kids. Or our parents might just be too tired to play with us. Above all, a large number of kids had the collective benefit of having an assortment of siblings, which was a lot less boring in our view than a family with fewer kids. Understandably, smaller families potentially had fewer disasters. If you're in the right frame of mind, though, disasters could be kind of fun.

One thing you could count on, however, was the fact that kids growing up in these big families, often run by parents putting on a zone defense instead of a man-to-man defense, was the growing sense of independence as each kid got older. We wouldn't wait for someone to do things for us and so we would figure it out for ourselves.

Our situation was a bit of an anomaly in Racine because it seemed like the rest of our neighbors and classmates actually came from families that put a little more thought into the child-rearing process. Back in suburban Chicago, our neighbors had more wherewithal than those in Racine, which in my mind, meant they must have felt that they the right to judge, either acquired through status or money.

Our family stood out, jumping up and down, raising our hands with a "Judge me! Judge me!" way about us.

Not so much in Racine. The environment felt different and if people were judging us, they just didn't make it so obvious. They didn't call our mom on the phone asking her to stop mowing her own grass in a bikini top. They didn't get all pissed off when our ducks wandered off into their yard and laid eggs. In Chicago, perhaps a simple "thank you" for the sheer entertainment value of your neighboring clown family would have sufficed. In Racine, the neighbors were just quiet about their disapproval, if they cared at all.

Plus, maybe you need to have more money if you want more kids. And maybe those older siblings won't give a shit about the younger ones and might feel a little of well-developed resentment if they're expected to bear the burden of that extra bit of responsibility in babysitting or watching out for younger siblings in the family. Or maybe, as in our case, you'd just find a way to create controlled chaos with a lot of fun and kids who cared just enough about each other not to inflict permanent bodily injury.

Our family had the same twenty-four hours in a day that every other family had, but with a larger group of kids. Who do you think is getting better care? I once ended up at the dentist with almost half a tooth gone to decay, not because there was an outright neglect situation going on in our house, but scheduling doctor and dentist appointments for six kids and their working parents is a second full-time job. Getting to those appointments was, of course, another hurdle. Add to that school, extra-curricular activities, and neighborhood kids coming and going at any given time, and you might imagine the effort needed to maintain any form of a schedule.

Our parents were married when our mom was only seventeen years old and fresh out of high school. They wasted little time in having kids and eventually had five of their own, fostering another, and adopting the last one—me.

The family line-up went like this. Timothy Patrick was born in 1959. He was creative and goofy in a fun and likeable way. He was hard-working and confident around girls and so he was never short of love interests. Tim started working at an ice-cream store before he was even old enough or tall enough to get a good reach into the ice cream freezers. He took after our mom's Scottish lineage in appearance.

Next, Marjorie Colleen, who was named after our maternal grandmother only because Dad got Mom to agree to it when she was drugged up during labor in 1960. Margie had a great big, friendly smile and bright green eyes. She was called Margie and hated it when we called her Marge. Without fail, she was always there to offer a maternal helping hand and without fail, not a single one of her brothers ever appreciated it. I did. I still do.

After Margie was John McGown, born in 1962. Having mostly Irish and somewhat Scottish kids meant paying homage to the "Mc or Mac" lineage twice. John viewed the world through a very different lens and had a small group of close friends his whole life. He built forts and motorcycles and cars and loved movie trivia and history. Like Margie, he was named after one of Mom's parents by an enthusiastic new dad who didn't take the time to run it by his spouse. John was tragically smart, in the sense that he had talents and intelligence that meant he could do just about anything with his life, but didn't. He lived an average life that was marginally happy due to a crushing dependence on alcohol.

Then two years later came Patrick O'Shean, who was the boy star among the junior high school girls at Sacred Heart, landing a lead in the *Pied Piper* play. He was the picture of an Irish poster child in appearance, looking more fair and freckled and more "McDonough" than the others. Patrick was funny, creative, and full of potential that was sidetracked for different reasons over the years.

Fast forward to 1967. Morgan Michael barely made it out of the hospital due to a battle between our mother's Rh-negative factor blood and her baby's incompatible Rh-positive blood. Morgan made a few return cameos to the ER in his early years for infant pneumonia, later as a toddler after pulling his little self into a bath filled with scalding hot water, and fast-forward to his kid-self with near deadly anaphylactic shock after a wasp attack. He managed to survive just fine. He was the kid who grayed his parents' hair by having the most repeated brushes with death.

Pulling in eighteen months after Morgan and at the end of the line was me, Kathleen Mary. Brown hair, brownish skin, brown eyes. Nothing particularly or obviously Irish about me other than the strong environmental affiliation and the constant feeling that I didn't quite fit in with the rest of the family. I was an outsider looking into a group of five kids who had a lot of things in common that I simply didn't share. When feeling optimistic, on some days, the differences made me feel special, although I was never really sure how or why.

Feeding six kids required a one-pot meal-approach, even with a dad who was a classically trained chef. He stuck to the basics like soup, spaghetti, chili, beef stew, and more soup, since anything above that would be a waste of money coupled with a lack of appreciation. There was no real upside to a chef making fancy meals for a bunch of kids. No kid was ready and waiting at the table with an "ooh" or an "ahh" over Beef Wellington or flaming Cherries Jubilee. We just didn't get it. Sometimes, he even made home-made macaroni and cheese, which far and away is better than the stuff in the box. But not when it comes to kids. The more processed, the better.

Growing up around someone with madly serious knife skills at home was a gift, especially when it came to our dad. I'd sit next to him and stare while he chopped and chopped and chopped on a huge wooden cutting board that slid out from under the counter and went back into its slot when you were done with it. If you were diligent, it would be washed, and even sanitized on occasion. But six kids and two adults meant twenty-four meals a day, and there's only so much time in the day, of course. Corners needed to be cut. Without knowing it, we were all learning to cook via immersion at the hands of a classically trained master whose meals we never truly gave the appreciation they deserved.

Our mom, who probably did love and appreciate his cooking, was put in charge of clean up. Not such a great deal. Anyone who has been around chefs knows that while creative, they can be a bit of a disaster when it comes to maintaining cooking stations, which in our situation meant the entire kitchen. Our dad would leave behind a tornado of onion skins, potato peels, dirty utensils, pots, and pans. It seemed that the number of dirty utensils tended to multiply when he was not happy with his wife.

Sometimes, maybe on those days when we were really bad, Mom would be the one to cook and we'd get tuna fish casserole, one of the oddest concoctions you could imagine. At the same time, the meal had an oddly satisfying and addictive feel to it. Noodles, canned mushroom soup, with canned tuna fish and of course, canned corn. Canned corn. The brownish mushy kind. Not that fancy frozen stuff. It was like an unholy alliance of ingredients, but a remarkably economical meal actually featuring seafood that fed a lot of kids on a couple of dollars.

Looking back, such meals were a little difficult to comprehend, because we were living in the land of milk and honey, fresh produce all around, farms and more farms, but canned stuff at the Wisconsin grocery stores was always both abundant and cheap.

Fortunately, every once a while, we would have a reprieve, which meant a trip to McDonald's, where my brothers decided the best combination of food ever was a Big Mac plus Filet-O-Fish, affectionately referred to as surf-and-turf. To me, it seemed the most disgusting concept ever imagined and as time went by, my culinary instincts proved to be sound.

Even more fortunate than our opportunities for occasional jaunts to the world of fast food was the fact that our brother Tim, the ever-industrious sibling, managed to score a job at Ponderosa Steak House. He was offered a job washing dishes, but knew his way around a grill and insisted on proving himself as a cook. He did and was promoted as a line cook while still in high school.

Years later, a French employer sent him to France for immersion training in their way of cooking, because he was the type of guy who created his opportunities through hard work and a likeable spirit.

Back at Ponderosa, impressed with his dedication, Tim's boss invited his family for dinner on the house for our brother's birthday. Big mistake, Ponderosa. All eight of us piled into the family station wagon with empty bellies. We ate and ate and ate, as our dad used to say: "Like we were going to the chair." Not surprisingly, we were not invited back.

One benefit to having many siblings is that the more kids around, the less likely it is that you might get caught doing something really bad. You could blend in and do a lot of taboo stuff while your older brothers were doing things that were far worse, like blowing things up with TNT they found by the railroad tracks, or throwing firecrackers at passing cars, or stealing candy from the dime store. So who cared about your relatively petty crimes.

There was a bit of an honor system approach to inter-sibling beatings, too. You could screw with your siblings and do really bad things to them, but you wouldn't dare go to Mom. Tattling usually meant more yelling and payback that was much worse than the problem of getting beat up in the first place. Still, everyone has his or her limits when it comes to being picked on by the same person every day.

My brother Morgan, not even two years older than me, found in me a much weaker sibling who wasn't especially fast, but who was also a bit too much of a wiseass. I was "Kathleen the (*string*) bean that (*really should have been who, but ok*) ate Racine." So my smart mouth meant that I got my butt kicked by Morgan—a lot.

For him, it had to be especially satisfying to kick my butt when Morgan himself was constantly getting beat up on by Patrick, who was three years older and clearly capable of overpowering him, just as Morgan could easily overpower me, pin me down, and annoy me to no end.

Our honor code meant that torturing a younger sibling only went so far. So one day, after suffering what seemed like hours of slaps to the head, the torture of being held down while Morgan dangled a long, nasty string of phlegm over my head, I had had it. That was it.

I was at the end of my seven-year-old rope. I went out and enlisted the older siblings for help and to exact my well-deserved revenge. And they knew, as the youngest in the family, I really had a void in my life—no underling to beat up on.

Then the older siblings corralled Morgan and brought him down to the basement. His cruelty had to stop. And the only way to stop sibling cruelty is to serve up a big heaping dose of much more exacting cruelty. Whether it was Pat, John, and Tim or some combination of the three (God knows, our peace-loving Margie would never have had anything to do with it)...they strung him upside down and handed me the darts. Not the nice, forgiving plastic darts you see these days, but the medieval ones with the extra-sharp, tetanus-causing metal tips.

I threw as hard and fast as I could and I won't lie, it was one of the best days of my childhood. Revenge was sweet and swift and so deserved.

And then, I ran. I ran and ran until I couldn't even tell where I was. It was the day when a little kid could take off wandering through the neighborhood without a thought of abduction or getting lost somehow. I knew I had to make myself scarce for a long time and it would be a matter of hours before Morgan came back down from a high-flying rage. It was a matter of survival and I knew that even with my limited number of years, I was on the lam and knew exactly what I needed to do to escape what I knew would be some pretty fierce retribution.

Just a few years before, Morgan accidental-ly" hit me over the head with a nine iron after I "accidentally" ruined his sandcastle in the sandbox. Blood poured down my face from every vantage point like a high school kid at prom in the movie *Carrie*. Mom raced me to the ER in our rickety station wagon.

Whether our siblings' type of aggressive physical behavior was directly proportional to the number of *Tom & Jerry* cartoons or *Three Stooges* episodes we watched as kids will never be known. But it is a distinct possibility. Some-one in those cartoons was always getting the short end of blunt force in one form or another, blown up by TNT, getting hit over the head with a vase, chair, or two-by-four. Understandably,

Morgan might have thought that a nine iron over the head would be perfectly fine, a little cartoon bump and that was it. This was part of the TV culture we loved, after all. Whatever the cause, though, I knew better and did my best to avoid a repeat.

I don't remember coming back home or when I saw Morgan after that. Either he got the message and was fearful of another "Come to Jesus" with the older siblings, or he somehow didn't realize I had been behind the Morgan-as-dartboard beating. Plus, the delivery method for the beating wasn't much different than other ones.

In our family, picking a weapon was more a matter of convenience than forethought. If there was a boiling-hot tea bag nearby, it could be flung at you without a thought. Lipton tea bags just pulled out of scalding water are better weapons than you'd think, because they stick to the skin while burning it.

If a wooden block or a sharp toy was handy, you knew to keep your mouth shut, or you'd find that thrown at your face, too. When we switched over to public schools in future years, knowing when to avoid conflict helped me avoid ass-kickings.

With the boys, there was also the occasional BB gun war, which was a bit more on the even side because at least Morgan, Pat, and John each had guns of equal caliber. They would run through the yard, using bushes and trees for cover. Of course, BB guns were more dangerous than average household weapons but miraculously, not one of the boys or their friends lost an eye. Maybe the prayers of our young Father Mike helped, after all.

BB guns were fair game just about everywhere in Wisconsin because anyone living out in the county or close to woods was packing something much more powerful than a weak little BB gun. Dads, uncles, and older brothers were out there hunting with some serious shotguns. What was the big deal if we were using BB guns for human target practice, anyway? Plus, it was friendly fire and that's ok in most sibling war rules of engagement.

In retrospect, while the beatings continued, they were just a way of life and in some cases, helped relieve life's frustrations in a not-so-positive way.

Danger, Danger Everywhere

THE SIX OF US HAD A FAIR APPRECIATION of the fact that life can be dangerous. Any attorney who has practiced law as a personal injury, medical malpractice, or product liability lawyer can certainly tell you that. Life is a tournament of risks.

As a parent, you can minimize some risks by reading warning labels or putting up safety gates or inserting special pieces of plastic to protect kids from jamming pieces of metal in outlets and electrocuting themselves. Or you could always just take a chance and save some money while doing it.

Life is also a matter of chance, isn't it? For every risk you think you might be protecting yourself against, there's another one that you don't have any clue about that might be much worse. Sleep on that.

In our household, a delicate balance prevailed between barely managed revolts to near-death experiences. An actual tournament bracket published by a major news outlet showed that you really didn't have to worry about serious injury or death from a shark attack. While they sound pretty awful and violent and getting attacked would be a hell of a way to end a nice beach vacation, you are far more likely to be injured by falling off a toilet seat. This doesn't seem right, but it is.

Most people don't typically put themselves in a shark's environment that often. Not even divers or snorkelers on vacation. If they are around sharks, they are at least looking for them and taking some precautions.

Toilet seats—just the opposite. Frequent contact, less precaution, more injuries.

The kids in our house seemed to make a hobby out of turning the benign into dangerous. It was usually inexpensive and made life just a lot more interesting in our own tournament of risks.

The dangers we encountered on a daily basis in our home and our environment were not just about the not-so-hidden dangers of excessive cigarette smoking or exploding gas tanks. The boys in the family were especially gifted with the sort of imagination that meant even the most honest appliance or tool or thing went missing because it was being used for a nefarious, new purpose. Somehow, we escaped grievous bodily harm and more importantly, managed not to hurt any of the innocent bystanders who entered and exited our house and yard on a daily basis. It was nothing short of a Christmas miracle.

Our mom, the chief historian in the telling of the "McDonough brushes with death," reveled in the telling her danger stories montage before a crowd. This usually took place during family gatherings at the holidays. There was the "Remember that time Pat fell out the second-story window when he was three?" story, to "Do you remember when John found dynamite by the train tracks and brought it to grammar school?" to "Hey, remember when the parakeet flew into the box fan—there were feathers everywhere??!" to a room full of guffaws, and so it would go. "Let's not forget the time Kathleen walked with her older siblings on her first day of kindergarten on the wrong day!" And the "Can you believe the time Pat fell off the couch and broke his arm and the doctor at the emergency room actually asked him how it REALLY happened?"

All of these situations, in retrospect, became kind of funny over the years. We had to have a sense of humor about it all.

When I got older and had three children of my own, I sometimes found myself wondering: "What kind of f'...in' crazy house was that, anyway??"

The unintended consequence of growing up in a household that boldly supported self-reliance was regular encounters with danger. Sending a kid down the street to buy cigarettes, letting a first-grader walk to school alone, or allowing kids to be out all day completely unsupervised meant those kids might get hurt. In our house, we had daily fight club events and were totally ok with the possibility of a confrontation of some kind outside of our perimeters. We felt that we had sufficient training. We were anything but naïve.

Like it or not, parents like ours who were otherwise occupied with jobs or problems or the things needed to run a household of eight helped us all grow up to be adults capable of figuring things out on our own. It helped us grow up to be people not expecting to have things done for them. It helped us grow up to be like the rest of the kids around us—anything but entitled.

Who's Missing?

You might think that leaving a kid behind would be a terrifying thought to a parent. Our parents did a phenomenal job of taking such things in stride. Whether because you just lost track of them or completely forgot about a kid or even because you were distracted by something else—the thought is terrifying to modern-day parents. Not even for a second when it came to raising kids in Southeastern Wisconsin in the 1970s and '80s.

And even if losing track of a child should have been at least a little mortifying from a parental peer-pressure standpoint, it wasn't. Not in our family. We were uniquely situated, because our mom, from the very beginning, never gave a shit what anyone thought. And I mean anyone. From priests, to teachers, to other moms and dads, to in-laws or outlaws, Jackie McDonough did not give a second of any day to

those people and their unique forms of judgment. Hers was a gift. Dare you cross her, dare
you actually tell her to her face what you
thought, good luck to you.

Losing a kid in the neighborhood, or at a
party, or at a fair, or wherever, was not that big a
deal in our family. Whoever it was, he or she
always found a way back, completely unharmed
and totally unfazed.

Once, our mom managed to get all five kids
ready and dressed and in the car for some
special occasion, which was no small feat. The
problem was that there were six of us kids at
that time. I was an infant and had been left in the
highchair. Jackie was driving down the street
feeling pretty good about herself when she
realized: "Where's Kathleen??" As if as an
infant, I had already figured out a way to crawl
out of the house on a whim. She came back for
me and there I was, still in the highchair, smiling
away like a Labrador puppy wagging her tail to
greet the new day.

A couple of years later, a toddler still and completely buck-naked, as the story goes, I managed to take myself for a little walk down our street. I was found in the neighbor's back-yard playing all alone without a hint of distress. Remarkably—although I was returned to our house by the Highland Park, Illinois, police, who had been called by what must have been a very alarmed neighbor—no reports were made or charges or any problems to our family whatso-ever.

This nonchalant treatment had much to do with the fact that our dad made friends with everyone and anyone. As the father of four very adventurous boys known for getting into trouble, you have to wonder if this was an accident. He was friendly with the local police chief in particular, and so, whether this was sheer luck or not, it had certainly helped keep us on the good side of the law in Highland Park. Not so much in Racine.

In future years, the boys in the family would regularly face run-ins for things that were

previously overlooked or excused, riding dirt
bikes down city streets, launching bottle rockets
at kids in neighboring yards, throwing apples
from our trees at the neighbor's dog Ralphie
when he refused to stop barking all day long,
and so on. By and large, the types of harm any of
us got involved in was to property, and minor
property damage at that. Fortunately, inflicting
personal injury was out of the collective wheel-
house of the McDonough kids. To hurt people
physically and emotionally takes planning and
meanness and the lack of a good heart. My
siblings and I had good hearts—we always did.

Another instance of the temporarily lost
McDonough child phenomenon happened when
one of the boys got left behind. One warm,
sunny Saturday, we all drove to the northern-
most part of Racine County to go to what was
basically a massive flea market called Seven Mile
Fair. That was a bit of a misnomer because there
was nothing "fair" about being dragged to the
Seven Mile Fair as a kid. You hear "fair" and you
think, "Cool, cotton candy, and farm animals,
and rides!" Not even close.

Seven Mile Fair is a huge flea market that goes what seems like seven miles. The Seven Mile comes from the country road it sits on, after Three Mile, Four Mile, Five Mile … you get it. It's still there in present-day Racine County, though it may be different from the way I recall it in the late 1970s and early '80s. That's not to say I have any expectation of it actually having improved since being transformed into a kid-friendly venue.

That day, like many others spent at Seven Mile Fair, we wandered around aimlessly hoping to find something we were actually interested in—a trinket, a tchotchke, anything. After what seemed like hours, we came back to the family station wagon and left for home, hot, dusty, sweaty, sunburned, and happy to be leaving. Our dad started to drive home. But something wasn't right about the station wagon. It seemed to have more space. It didn't feel the same. We looked around and at each other, not quite realizing just exactly what it was that seemed different. We had just about made it to

Three Mile Road when someone yelled: "Hey, aren't we missing someone?"

We all looked around the car and it took us a bit, but we eventually figured out the youngest boy, Morgan, was missing. Finally, someone said in a rather calm voice: "Hey, where's Morgan?!?" The station wagon was quickly turned around and sped back to the Seven Mile Fair. Morgan was standing at the entrance with a candy apple in hand, swatting away bees in the blazing hot sun. I remember that candy apple clear as day. It's something none of us had ever had. It was always a caramel apple. He must have decided "What the hell. I'm all alone now, time to start living my life."

We pulled up to the entrance, Morgan got into the car unceremoniously, and told us all, "I knew you'd come back for me eventually." He said it in the sweetest and most matter-of-fact way you could ever imagine. And of course, we did come back for him.

I considered Morgan a major pain in the neck. He beat me regularly without managing to leave a mark, but was probably the most harmless of the bunch. That was the thing about my siblings; any bad decisions they made in life usually hurt themselves more than anyone. None of them were mean-spirited, especially not Morgan.

It was one of the few quiet rides I can remember with all of us in the car. No one dared say a word. Not even a single "When are we gonna get there?!?" complaint, cleverly disguised as a question.

Kids who accidentally get left behind learn a thing or two about paying attention. First, you start to become a lot better about keeping up with the rest of your crew. Second, if you don't, and that can happen to a kid as we learned repeatedly in our family, you damned well better know how to spend a couple of hours entertaining yourself in a strange place like a flea market or fair, because it may be a while before the search party comes back for you.

Not Like the Others

In Racine in the 1970s and '80s, it wasn't all that common to come across kids who had been adopted. Adoptees were was sort of a weird novelty, like being one of a handful of minorities in an all-white town. People would talk about the situation like it was completely normal in front of the adopted kid, as if the child wasn't there. "OH! He's adopted! Oh, my gosh, that's so cute!"

There were plenty of reasons you didn't find many adopted kids.

First, private adoptions cost money and for the most part, the town wasn't known for people with a lot of expendable income. The place we had just moved away from—the North Shore of Chicago—was where rich people lived and were more likely to adopt. Not so much the blue-collar crew. There may have been tiny little circles of the wealthy and well-connected in Racine, but those were places in the social strata I never appreciated or understood as a kid.

I distinctly remember asking one of my high school classmates what he meant when he said "That BMW is a really sweet ride." I had never even heard of a BMW. He looked at me like I was a complete idiot and apparently I was when it came to luxury vehicles. There weren't exactly a lot of "sweet rides" in our city.

Second, most people didn't give their kids up for adoption because "keeping up with the Joneses"—whether in terms of image or the size of your posse— really wasn't a thing. Few people really got involved in their neighbors' business. They were too busy keeping their regular jobs and paying the bills to stop and make comparisons in our neighborhood. There was even an unverified rumor in town that at least one of the local high schools ranked in the top five amongst U.S. high school teen pregnancies, and that the high school girls banded together in keeping the statistic alive.

So where did the money for an adoption come from in our case? Our great-grandma died, apparently. There was a bit of an inheritance that was spent immediately on two somewhat related items: 1) an addition to our increasingly smallish home in Illinois; and 2) adopting a kid.

Our parents had been at a party when a friend of a friend told them about an upcoming private adoption, and so timing and a random inheritance made our family of five kids into six. Our parents simply loved kids, who brought joy to an imperfect marriage.

I was the only one of our clan who happened to be adopted. I didn't look anything like the rest of the family. My brothers and sisters were fair and freckled with undisputedly Irish features. Not me. Brown eyes, no freckles, olive skin. Sunscreen either hadn't been invented yet or we just didn't use it, so every time we spent a day at the lake, I was the only one who came back with a dark tan and zero evidence of a sunburn.

That in itself is weird, because people never really pointed out those very visible differences to us. Adults were probably being polite. The kids didn't notice. I didn't notice. Noticing differences in appearance and skin color is learned and thankfully, we were never taught.

Our mom told me as an adult that she "thought" she told me I had been adopted at an early age. That is, our parents told me really "cute" stories about how a beautiful young Native American woman left me in a basket on their doorstep one cold winter day. To me, that was a really sweet and imaginative story narrated to make me feel "special." And yet, despite what should absolutely have been obvious to me, I had no clue.

Meanwhile, my brothers took a slightly different approach about my adoption origins with cute, little vignettes like: "We found you by the railroad tracks," or "We found you in a garbage can." It didn't strike me that these sorts of comments had anything at all to do with

131

adoption. I just thought they were a joke until I learned otherwise.

One day, when I was nine years old in the summer between third and fourth grade, Morgan and I ran into someone who mistakenly put his private life out in the open and admitted he was adopted. In fact, the more likely event was that we were with other kids who were talking about another kid, who was adopted. We continued walking home, talking about how weird it would be to be adopted. And we walked in through the garage, through the very muddy mud room, and up the back stairs into the kitchen. Our mom was sitting at the small kitchen table, cigarette in hand, and an ashtray getting perilously close to an overflow.

"Guess what?" Morgan announced, in what was probably an annoying and overly confident tone.

"What?" she answered, unfazed and uninterested.

"Jimmy is ADOPTED!" Morgan told her in a way that he probably meant to convey as scandalous. I have no idea if this was the kid's name, but it's a solid placeholder.

"Well, Kathleen's adopted," she responded, in a completely matter-of-fact sort of way.

Dead silence followed. Morgan and I stood there, frozen, looking at one another, stunned. Neither one of us had a clue. It was a memory that is so impressed on my brain that I remember the little things that surrounded it, because my ears were ringing and I felt like someone else standing there, listening to conversation between strangers in my own home.

It so happened that I had just bought the latest and greatest in kid's candy products, and had a massive wad of orange-flavored *Bubble-Yum* bubble gum in my mouth. Without an ability to respond in any way whatsoever, I stood there, frozen in the middle of the kitchen for what seemed like an eternity. The sickeningly sweet orange syrup dripped down my throat. I wanted to cry, but I felt more like an idiot than anything.

Really? How could I not have known this? How did I not figure this out somehow on my own? There were clues everywhere. Just exactly how stupid and oblivious was I? Not even the repeated comments from the peanut gallery of brothers pointing out my differences over the years seemed to dawn on me.

And then for a brief moment, I thought: *"Holy shit! Maybe all those stories about where they found me weren't just stories after all?!? In a garbage can?! What?"*

Within a few moments, our mom gave me what she thought was a better, or at least a decent, explanation of how things had gone down and that I really, truly was adopted. I had not been found on the side of the road or on the train tracks or not even delivered by a beautiful Native American woman with long black braids, leaving me in a basket on our front steps. Instead, I learned that I had a young biological mother who couldn't keep me.

From that point on, I took decidedly different approach to life. No more surprises, no more looking—or worse, feeling like an idiot. Investigate everything. Listen carefully to the adult conversations down below from the top of the stairs on the second floor. Walk on tippy-toes so the floorboards don't creak and the older siblings or parents had no idea you are listening in.

Over time, there must have been all sorts of things I really wished I hadn't heard. But you have to take the good with the bad, and knowing just about every piece of gossip and learning about assorted problems wasn't too terrible from a kid's perspective.

For years, I felt that I was not only different from my siblings in appearance, but that I was just different. From all of them. And that I didn't belong.

* * *

I later learned that I had a very loving birth mother, who happened to be a college student with an incredibly controlling mother who would never have permitted a tarnish to her imaginary social status that an out-of-wedlock child might bring.

Eventually, I met my birth mother and her family, as well as my birth father and his family. Until I had my own family, more than anyone, I needed my birth mother in my life. She had four children of her own and lived a few hours away in Iowa and was the kindest and most patient soul I'd ever met. She gave me every possible manner of affirmation and support I could have hoped for, without knowing I ever needed it or hoped for it in the first place.

Some navigating was needed between the family I grew up knowing, my birth mother's family, and my birth father's family. I had a sense of not belonging hovering close to belonging at times, until the day my first child was born. Then, my own nuclear family meant I knew exactly where I was meant to be. Wisconsin became our weekend getaway as semi-permanent residents. We wandered throughout the state with all its woods and farms and lakes as visitors, which meant we belonged and didn't belong there, either. Then it didn't matter, because wherever we were, we belonged together.

"Wait! You Go to Church?"

WHEN WE MOVED FROM THE largely Jewish Highland Park, Illinois area to Racine, Wisconsin, the change was palpable even to me as a six-year-old in 1975. In Highland Park, being Catholic was my "secret," and I kept the fact that I "went to church" with "people who took Communion" hidden from my non-Christian classmates. Kids don't like standing out. So if you had something about you that made this happen, you hid it.

I once found out one of my closest friends in Highland Park was Catholic like me and it blew me away. I remember telling her, and the few other kids who, like me, didn't have a Bat Mitzvah in my future: "Wait! You go to CHURCH?!?!" in a "no f'ing way!!" kind of tone.

I thought no one was as nutty as our family and somehow the translation of "crazy family" to me meant Irish or Catholic. It turns out, though, that our particular religion or nationality had little or nothing to do with how things went down in our house. Our family dynamic was a combination of random facts and events and people.

Our family was not at all typical of anything, really. You could say "typical Irish Catholic family," but our mom, Jackie, always hated Catholicism ("all that goofy guitar music") and she wasn't even really Catholic. She was a mostly Scottish Protestant who converted to Catholicism when she married our dad, much to the chagrin of her grandparents, who apparently banned the wedding and refused to attend.

As far as religion goes, Jackie was not particularly religious. On Sundays, she helped get us all dressed and ready for church, but that was mostly to appease our dad. No one wants to be called out for being "unreligious." And the fact that our parents got all six of us to church on time was nothing short of a miracle, unless you count the promise of Honey Bear Pancakes after church part of that miracle.

The Protestant thing makes sense though. As kids, we always saw our mom as the distant figure who provided for us as a parent, but wasn't about to fawn over us or smother us with affection. Far from it. The boys seemed to function just fine within this arrangement, while Margie and I probably had a more romanticized and unfair expectation of what a mom should be like. Ours no doubt worked hard to pay the bills and provide for us generally and always had dinner ready like clockwork. It would be some sort of meat and vegetable and starch, or the one -pot meals, like chili, soup, beef stew, or something like that. But she wasn't the "get down on your hands and knees" and "play with the kids in the sandbox" type. In a way, she was forced to take on what most people viewed to be the typical dad role: provider and disciplinarian with very clear limits on acceptable behavior.

It could very well be that by the time the youngest kids were growing up, she was just tired. She had suffered her share of tragedy, sadness, and disappointment, so fatigue was quite natural. Since older siblings were around, they were expected to pick up the slack. Our mom kept the household and attended to our basic needs, but kids were expected to find things to do, even if we told her repeatedly throughout the summer: "I'm bored, there's nothing to do." Those were the days well before parents planned out every waking moment of their kids' days. We entertained ourselves and if there were sports teams, parents weren't exactly lining the stands.

When our mom eventually became a grandmother, it was sort of like "Well, I've done that. No, thank you." and she stayed the course with her grandchildren. Pleasant, nice, still a bit distant in a way that only a Protestant could understand. Protestant, never really Catholic, never truly converted.

Over time, our mom developed many other reasons to simply not like the Catholic church. There was that "goofy guitar music" and singing at our Catholic church that annoyed her. More likely, it may have started when Catholic Charities allowed the family to foster and fall completely in love with a baby, then unceremoniously taking him from us two years later. It didn't get any better later when down on her luck as a single mom, our mom was pressured to donate more money to the local Catholic church, the same one that told her that she was not welcome to receive Holy Communion or remarry because her Catholic husband divorced her.

* * *

Before they got married, our parents were next-door neighbors from a small town in north-central Illinois. Our dad came from a very large family, nine kids in all, in what seems to have been a circus-like environment. He had twin older brothers, then came our dad Tom, and then sixteen years later, his parents decided to have six more kids. Two of the younger children died young, one from complications of extreme Down's Syndrome and another in a car accident at age seventeen. The death of one child is unthinkable. Two, indescribable. And then the patriarch sadly and suddenly died in his fifties from a heart attack in his sleep, leaving a trail of broken-hearted kids. It was thought that a lethal combination of stress, alcohol, and heart disease took him. It could have been as simple as a broken heart.

Our dad, in spite of all he had been through, was the eternal optimist. The type of positive, happy-go-lucky sort of guy who didn't think it particularly important to worry about the future. You can't control it anyway. He had a slew of one-liners and funny comments that either cracked us up or resulted in eye-rolls once they attained an overused status:

- "She fell out of the ugly tree and hit every branch on the way down!"

- "When you live well, you naturally ascend to the top!" (Usually when he found a good parking spot).

- "Don't you ever die!" (When he'd look in a mirror, with an audience of a kid or two nearby, and make a goofy face).

- "You'll be sorry, when I'm out on Boot Hill…"

- "Why don't you go outside and play with the traffic."

- "Put a couple of eggs in your shoe…and beat it!"

As a dad, he was fun, funny, and silly and when you were with him, made you feel like you were his best friend, with a very big emphasis on the "when you were with him" part. As a friend, he was much more reliable. He wasn't the dad most kids need; he was the dad most kids want. He was the dad your friends loved and couldn't understand why you weren't perfectly enamored with him at every level.

Our dad was good at many things. He made life so much fun and looked at the bright side, always. But he was not so good at discipline and consistency, which can lead to bad results when it comes to raising children. He never held a grudge and few people, if anyone, I ever met held a grudge against him. It was impossible. He just didn't have the strength to stay mad or have people mad at him, for that matter. He was one thousand percent Irish, so blarney was part of his everyday reality.

When he was a kid, he was known as "Red" for his ruddy, freckled skin and reddish hair. He was a living leprechaun. Mischievous, fun, and hard to catch. A few times he even dressed up as one for the Chicago St. Patrick's Day parade, green glitter, short suit, white tights and all, handing out dozens of green carnations to the ladies in the crowd. He loved making others feel better about themselves, even though he never felt as good as he should have about his own self. An imaginary life as a leprechaun would have made much more sense than the life he ended up with, after all.

Our mom's upbringing and home life were pretty much the opposite of her Irish-Catholic husband's. Her mother graduated from North-western University in 1926 to be rewarded with a career as an executive assistant in which men typically reaped the benefit of her intelligence. Much to our grandmother's dismay, our mom avoided post-secondary education entirely. She had only one sibling, a brother a decade older, who later went on to become a member of the faculty in the UC-Berkeley chemistry department.

Rather than follow a path of college or a career, our mom fell in love with the boy next door. The first thing she did after graduating from high school was to get married in early June in 1956, before she even had the chance to reach the age of majority. Children were soon to follow.

Her new husband, our dad, was barely twenty-three and had recently returned from the service as an Army Staff Sergeant in the Korean War. He was fun and creative, not at all interested in any fighting or war, and ended up becoming a cook. He came back to Chicago and continued this interest by attending chef's school.

Our parents had a baby boy and over the next ten years, had four more children, fostered a sixth by the name of Arnie Gonzalez for almost three years, and later adopted me.

As for Arnie, legend has it that as a toddler, Arnie tried to pull the legs off one of our turtles and eat them. Other than that blip in his childhood development, Arnie was pretty much a perfect little boy who happened to be of Puerto Rican descent. This fact didn't matter to anyone in our family, but it played a role with the institution in charge of placing him in our home. When he was about three, Catholic Charities, which had to have realized our family was pretty obviously "white" when our parents took

147

him in as an infant, decided he needed to be relocated to another home because suddenly our family was "too white."

A few years later, they adopted me at five days old. I was a brownish baby, certainly browner than any of their biological children, but not technically "brown," as in the Census' definition of brown or Hispanic.

Country-Club Ways

WITH A SOLID BACKGROUND IN THE culinary arts and a gift for gab, our dad was soon promoted from chef to country club manager. The role of a country club manager in the U.S. is a job that is kinda-sorta white collar, because for years, male managers wore suits and ties at all times, and women managers wore dresses or something similarly business-like, and in fact, many still do. This strikes me as odd, because the whole idea behind a country club is that it is a place where wealthy people go to relax, to golf, to swim, not to wear suits or business attire, or to be around others who do.

Perhaps the whole concept itself doesn't make a lot of sense, really. Though country clubs are decidedly social in nature, they are where scores and scores of deals are made on golf courses and in the private dining room.

Those who don't belong may never know they don't stand a chance because they weren't in the room where things happened.

Fortunately for our dad, you didn't need a college degree to be a club manager, but you would need to know a thing or two about the kitchen and the "back of the house" to make sure country-club members felt like they were getting their money's worth. At the same time, a country club manager position was also a position squarely within the blue-collar service industry.

Dad went from high school straight into the military during escalating conflicts in Asia. He became an Army cook during the Korean War, largely because he would have been the last person to engage in any conflict of any kind—on the field or in his personal life. There was something in his genetic makeup that made him conflict-averse to the extreme, which meant that he engaged in a bit of the white-lie blarney from time to time. He came back to Chicago and went to culinary school. His first job out of the Army was as a chef at the Drake Hotel on Michigan Avenue. Our dad then worked at a few country clubs on Chicago's North Shore until the move to Racine.

On Mondays, when the Racine Country Club was closed and members took the day off, we kids invaded the club with reckless abandon like a bunch of hooligans. The club's doors were shut, staff went home to rest, and Lord knows where the members went or whether this was even an allowable thing. In fact, it wasn't. With no one else around, all six of us were allowed to come and use the pool, or golf, or eat at the snack bar, or violate all sorts of rules. We snuck around the pool knowing we didn't really belong, but on hot summer days we didn't care. We just wanted access to a pool, any pool. We didn't even have central air in our home, for God's sake. And we wanted soda, snacks, and all sorts of other things we probably didn't deserve. Kids want what they want. They don't think much about it. It's that simple.

Sometimes we could bring friends, and, if you were a favored employee, you'd get an invite, too. The only real supervision over a country club manager was the president of the board, and since that person was also a member, the president wasn't allowed on club premises on Mondays either. The *Caddy Shack* club environment was not much of a stretch and if you had a manager lacking discipline or availing himself of certain privileges, it was pretty unlikely that anyone would ever find out. If your employees also fell for your blarney, well, there was not much concern about self-policing either.

Ultimately, the lack of discipline in the country club setting did us in and it was suggested that our dad work elsewhere. He had taken up with a twenty-one-year-old pantry girl, a job title for a person who makes salads and appetizers for events or dinners. Maybe he loved her or maybe he didn't, but this seems to have played a role in his move back to the Chicago suburbs. Apparently, the president of the board could put up with a lot of things, and so could the employees, but a line was drawn when it was discovered the club manager was cheating on the mother of his six children right across the street from their very home.

The day our dad sat us down to give us news of the ultimate divorce, he told us we were having a family meeting after dinner. This was weird to all of us, because we never had family meetings *per se*, and we didn't really know what this was supposed to look like. We thought it may have been another one of his silly pranks. My brothers laughed and joked: "Ohhhh, big deal. Big family meeting, right?"

We didn't take much of anything very seriously at our house because that just wasn't the tone. If you tried to be serious, well, you were pretty much ridiculed for it.

Not this day. After dinner, we all sat around the family dining room table and the conversation started with my dad telling us all: "Some things are going to change, and some things will stay exactly the same. You're all still going to have three square meals a day…" and then it was like we all sat there in a fog, because we could see he kept talking but none of it made any sense.

Then he told us he was leaving. I was nine years old and my little heart was broken and no doubt, everyone else felt the same way. Those of us who were old enough to know better, knew he was a terrible husband, but I was a kid, and kids who don't know their dad is a cheat, absolutely love all the fun and nonsense and so to me, I was losing a huge part of my life, all in an instant.

Fortunately, a variety of positive tradeoffs came over the years. Kids with divorced parents want things to stay the same but this is a life lesson. Things rarely do. Kids can control some things but there are many more that are outside of their reach. The six of us knew things were not going to be the same normal, but we got used to it and adapted.

The first big tradeoff was that we would have to split holidays and birthdays with our parents. The bright side was that later that year, I was given what any young girl craved: a blowout birthday party at Shakey's Pizza. It was child bribery at its finest and only a temporary fix to how pissed off I felt at my parents for doing something that would surely be noticed. I was the winner, so I felt that at least for the time being, we were vindicated and victory over my classmates' nuclear families was all mine, even if only for a day.

That same year, we also had one of the most memorable Christmas present extravaganzas ever, with boatloads of presents the family clearly couldn't afford but as kids, we sure as heck weren't going to say a word.

Post-Apocalyptic Family

EVENTUALLY, WE SETTLED ON THE new normal, which in kids of divorced parlance language translates to "this stinks." Mostly, because it meant massive changes in a kid's life and the whole "resilient kid" thing may or may not be true, but the initial adjustment felt like wearing uncomfortable shoes. The more positive siblings—as in the annoyingly positive kids—came to the conclusion that running back and forth between two homes that have no semblance of the other is a fun and interesting way of life. It took us a while to get to that point.

Our dad's new job at another country club meant non-member Mondays were still a thing, but only in the summer if we were down to visit him for long weekends in south suburban Chicago. Usually, we spent about one weekend a month with him, hanging out in the "19th Hole," a bar and grill adjacent to the golf course.

Morgan and I played pool, dined on decadent things we could not possibly have appreciated at the time: shrimp cocktail and prime rib with fresh, warm sourdough bread loaded with all the butter we wanted, hot fudge sundaes, bottomless glasses of soda pop. We behaved well to avoid notice and stayed in the grill or in the back of the kitchen. It seemed like we were always waiting for our dad; he worked a lot and had the sort of job in which he was expected to be available at all times.

In a way, the kitchen staff doubled as our babysitters. The club had a chef named Mr. Lou Wing, who had managed to escape communist China and Mao Tse Tung's reign and ended up in the Chicago suburbs. He was a talented cook and dedicated employee; he spoke decent English but had an incredibly hard-to-understand Cantonese accent. He was a small and energetic sprite and you just knew that he was a good soul.

Lou Wing had a few extended family members living nearby, although we all wondered whether he had lost his immediate family back in China. His face was old and wrinkled and his body looked worn and tired, but he still managed a huge smile when people spoke to him. Mr. Wing was one of those adults who came to life when kids were around. You knew he sincerely loved being around young people. His face had aged way beyond his years, and he had just a few yellow teeth dangling from the top of his gums.

When Mr. Wing wasn't too busy, he taught me to play blackjack and poker, along with some of the other kitchen staff. He would tell me: "After while, after while, we play poker." But at the time, it sounded more like "Up to why, up to why" and I nodded in agreement since I didn't really know what he was saying; I just wanted to play more cards. He spoke in such a happy and animated way that you wanted to hang around him.

Later in the day, the card games began and he'd give me a few bucks of seed money. As far as ten-years-olds go, I was becoming a decent card player. Forget the fact that the kitchen staff was also serving as my personal babysitter; I was having a ball. In the meantime, Morgan usually went down to the bar and grill perfecting his pool game.

The new country club had employee apartments and so Tim and Margie, both out of high school, went to live with our dad. Each managed to score their own apartment. For Tim and Margie, much like our dad, the initial stint in the Badger State was short-lived. As to their new living quarters, it seemed like a crazy setup.

The employee apartments were incredibly spartan and were occupied by a large group of lovable misfits. The complex was like a college dorm without a "resident advisor." There were stories of all-night parties with kegs. One time, a Golden Retriever helped himself to the dripping keg each time someone walked away from a pour. Later that night, when the dog went out to relieve himself, he lifted his leg to do his business on a bush, fell on his back, and peed all over himself.

John and Pat were soon to come after Tim and Margie to share that environment. The complete lack of planning or parental discipline inevitably led to a notable increase in pot and alcohol.

Lou Wing also lived in the complex, and after working twelve-hour days, he went back to his apartment, alone, minded his own business, and waited for the next day. It seemed his only enjoyments were work, his fellow employees, and the occasional little kids willing to play blackjack with him during his breaks.

We never found out his real backstory, because like many people you meet in life, you either don't want to pry or you don't want to bring up old wounds. What very little we know of Mr. Wing fascinated me. He had clearly suffered but remained immensely kind-spirited. He wouldn't harm a flea and was as sweet and gentle as a grandfather every kid wished they had.

Because our dad was so good at making other people feel special, he had a fairly loyal kitchen staff that followed him from place to place over the span of several decades. He would be fired or would quit and we never really got the real story in any case, but our sneaking suspicion was that alcohol and women likely played a role, every time. And thus it was that his girlfriend followed him to Illinois and Mr. Wing stayed with him for years.

Another loyal follower of our dad's was a middle-aged woman by the name of Ninna Anderson. Now living on her own, she had immigrated from Denmark to the U.S. Ninna was a teenager during WWII and played an active role in the Scandinavian Underground, responsible for transporting, hiding, and saving European Jews. She was like a grandma to us. Our maternal grandmother had long since passed away and our paternal grandmother was raising the younger end of her nine children. After having three boys, she and her husband chose to have six more kids, sixteen years later.

I loved Ninna with all my heart. Like Mr. Wing, she was kind and sweet and genuinely took an interest in our lives. She had no children of her own and largely lacked any reason whatsoever to develop any degree of patience or tolerance for little kids. She had old-fashioned-looking, wavy, blondish-grayish, short hair. She often laughed her loud, unobstructed laugh, each time revealing a few gold teeth in the back of her mouth . She had deep wrinkles and light blue eyes that reminded you of oceans far, far, away. She was the perfect grandma who wasn't a grandma, because she never had time for children of her own, or there was a story that none of us ever knew. She lived in a little apartment and used any money she made on world adventures, taking trips to every continent with a tour group she didn't even know. She was a complete badass, from my modern-day perspective. She lived on her own, supported herself, and answered to no one.

Ninna regularly took Morgan, Pat, and me on little outings all over town and once even drove us forty-five minutes away to Great America Amusement Park. The day was the

absolute best day! She had to have been in her
60s or even 70s by then, but she kept up with us
all over the park in her flesh-toned orthopedic
shoes, grayish-blond pin curls, hearing aids, and
rhinestone-studded granny glasses. We went
from ride to ride and then back to the same rides
again, and not once did she complain. Then,
exhausted from covering mile after mile at the
theme park, she took us for a late-afternoon
lunch at a cafeteria in the park and marched us
all straight past the cash registers, trays loaded
with food, to a table nearby to eat lunch.

Having survived the German occupation of
Denmark during WWII, Ninna concluded that
clearly the food and drink must be included in
the exorbitant cost of admission. But it wasn't,
and as a ten-year-old kid, I knew that well
enough. The entire rest of the day, I was petrified
that either the Great America police or worse, the
local police, would come find us and put us in
some sort of amusement park jail. Nauseous and
nervous, I was convinced authorities would
catch up with us and punish poor Ninna for

doing nothing more than treating a few kids to a great day.

Pat and Morgan, on the other hand, found the entire event something between hilarious and thrilling. Of course, they went back a few times for more, again walking right past the cashiers with trays full of burgers and fries they couldn't even finish. They were right, as it turned out. Nothing ever happened and the place was so filled with unmanaged sensory overload that the teenaged kids manning the cash registers could not care a penny about a group of goofy kids getting free food with a small but mighty Danish septuagenarian.

In fact, neither Pat nor Morgan ever seemed to worry about anything at all and suffered few repercussions for bad decisions or bad behavior. It was ridiculous. They did what they did and didn't care. As for Ninna, her difficult past had absolutely earned her the right to flout inconsequential amusement park rules and regulations.

Ninna joined our family for holidays and get -togethers, but the frequency of her visits diminished over time as we spread out and about and away from home, both physically and emotionally. We wrote to one another and kept in touch and she always knew, I hope, how special she was to our family. Ninna was one of those people who enters your life with an incredible backstory that like many, don't tell it either due to modesty or an unwillingness to revisit the pains of the past.

Another time, we were sent to go camping with some family members of our dad's pantry girl girlfriend. We drove north to the Wisconsin-Michigan border, set up camp with a tiny pop-up camper, and wandered about the campsite. The group consisted of Morgan, me, a girl a bit younger than us, and her parents. We soon realized the whole thing involved a bunch of folks in Northern Wisconsin drinking boatloads of booze with limited public shower access. Other families parked their crappy trailers around campfires and basically drank and ate processed foods all day.

The Saturday-night tradition included a wapatoolie (pronounced "wop-uh-two-lee") party, so the adults drove home in an especially hung-over state the next day. The party went something like this: early in the day, each group of campers brought a bottle of cheap liquor of any color, flavor, or alcohol content, which is then poured into a community cooler. Chopped oranges and cherries or whatever fruit was on sale at the local Piggly Wiggly grocery store were then added.

The boozy mix was allowed to ferment a few hours and ice was added just before the party began. Then, the adults swill the boozy sugar-bomb, getting completed plastered while the kids played nearby. Very Wisconsin, indeed, and a far cry from the "Club Monday" we had gotten used to over the past few years.

In college some years after that, I experienced a lazier version of the wapatoolie party—powdered drink mix plus grain alcohol—which led to equally troubling consequences.

It turned out that one of the girls from the campsite went to our grade school and was the really odd kid, in a way that let the rest of the world know that she really didn't care one bit if anyone thought she was odd. She relished it. She worked at it. She perfected it. Her strange behavior, smirks, unexpected and poorly timed snickers, rose to a level that struck fear in her classmates and those around her. She was unpredictable, unusual, and never went out of her way to make friends. When we got back to school, we did what any reasonable schoolkids would do—we acted as though we had never met.

Fortunately, Morgan and I toed the line while staying socially distant enough to not get invited back for another camping excursion, so in truth, it all worked out just fine. Being relatively young, we had a hard time silently expressing the disapproval of such situations. The look of disdain had to be all over my face, if not Morgan's as well. Mission accomplished; score one for the disenfranchised little ones.

Soon after the camping trip, we were invited by our dad's friend Ted to take a plane ride over Chicago. We anxiously awaited what we thought would be the greatest thing that ever happened in our short lives. Ted was one of those people everyone universally referred to as a "great guy." He was a polio survivor, gifted pianist, and amateur pilot.

Regarding the amateur pilot part, a parent might think twice about putting his kids on a small aircraft over a major metropolitan area. Not our dad. He never gave a second thought about the flip side of fun—the dangerous part. Up we went, way above Chicago, thrilled as could be, flying right over the Sears Tower itself. Then, as it often did, fun was met by reality and things came screeching to a halt—figuratively. The dreaded call came in from the nearest air tower. As it turns out, we were directly in the path of the Blue Angels' practice runs for the Chicago Air Show.

Morgan and I continued to go back and forth to visit our dad in Illinois as long as he held the job, which was more than a couple of years, this time. Tim or Margie was charged with driving Morgan and me the two hours each way. Every time we came back to Wisconsin, Morgan and I sat in the back seat of the old used Impala that smelled like mold and had only been used by "an old lady who drove it back and forth to church once a week." We held our noses when we saw the large Wisconsin-shaped wooden sign on the side of the highway: "Industry, Recreation, Industry, Agriculture." At some point, it said "Open for Business" as a sort of middle finger pointed toward Wisconsin's neighbor to the south; it was later changed back to a more friendly tone.

As our car raced back over the border, Morgan, Pat, and I held our noses and let out loud, audible "eeewwwss" hoping our protest would be noticed by an adult. We claimed it smelled the minute we crossed the state line into Wisconsin because we wanted to move away from the place where we first learned what it felt like to have our hearts broken.

* * *

We remained loyal to our Chicago sports teams even though the Chicago Cubs lost year after year. We proudly sang *Bear Down, Chicago Bears* each time the Blackhawks or the Bulls edged out the Milwaukee Admirals or the Bucks. Mostly, we did this because it got a rise out of the Wisconsin locals, without fail. There's no greater rivalry than Wisconsin and Illinois sports fans.

As an adult, I have the opposite reaction crossing back over into Illinois: a place with ridiculously high taxes and corruption to end all corruption. Nevertheless, it had a city I just couldn't seem to shake and where I eventually agreed to marry and raise three children.

* * *

Somehow our dad found a way to fit us into his busy life in Illinois. He was never alone, and always had a poor soul of a girlfriend or a friend nearby. We were mixed into the fabric of that life. Our dad was fun and crazy and unpredictable. He was "Disneyland Dad" on steroids.

His ability to attract and find random women over the years was nothing short of amazing. Was he the most attractive guy? Maybe not. Did he have a beer belly? Sure. Did he have six kids, alimony, and child support in arrears? Why, yes, he did. Receding hairline? Check that box, too. Still, the guy found a way to charm all sorts of gullible, wayward women. Or maybe he was the gullible, wayward one, but he never, ever gave up insisting that a woman was with him at all times.

Our dad's other life as a womanizer culminated with the woman he brought to Patrick's wedding. It wasn't a regular date, not at all. This time, he decided that rather than come alone, he would bring a blind date to his third son's wedding. It would have been perfectly acceptable for some member of our family to call him out for this somewhat rash decision. Yet, when it came time for friends and family members to stand up and give toasts and speeches, our mom and dad spontaneously got up, gave a toast to the new couple, and sang a cheerful song about a bicycle built for two as if nothing but happy things had ever happened between the two of them over the past thirty-odd years. At least the blind date had the common sense to lay low during the wedding, and she was never heard from again.

All Those Animals

SOME INDIVIDUALS ARE KNOWN to have high intelligence quotients (IQs), while others with high emotional quotients (EQs). There is a third and less appreciated group of individuals who exhibit a high AQ—the animal quotient. These are individuals who, no matter their age or status, have a better appreciation and under-standing of animals compared to other people.

Our family was high in AQ. We collected animals like tchotchkes. We knew a lot about animals because we had so many of them. We had typical rescue dogs and cats, adopted from animal shelters not as a social statement or a way to feel superior in our decisions, but because it was significantly less expensive than purchasing well-bred dogs.

The list of pets we acquired over the years goes on and on. We had parakeets, a mynah bird, bunnies, guinea pigs, hamsters, turtles, an aquarium full of fish and at some point, a pool with ducks. It was like we as kids came up with the most absurd animal requests of our parents just to see if we could get them to say "No. Not that one."

We kept lots of animals around the house and unless they got sick—which ours never really did—they didn't cost too much. If they got really sick, well, they died or they ran away.

Of course, there were the occasional dog pukes around the house, but nothing serious. That became a sort of game between all the brothers—they invented a contest about who could avoid the dog puke the longest. Could you walk around it and avoid the smell and the disgusting appearance for a few hours? For a day or so?

One day, someone brought home a "gag" vomit prank, the rubber type that sticks on the floor to mimic dog vomit. The problem was that it was so realistic, you were afraid to touch and it would sit there for hours or days, which was normal by "real" dog puke standards, because we'd never clean the real stuff up anyway. We would avoid it, pretend we never saw it, and then when our parents asked us why we hadn't cleaned it up, we had plausible deniability. Which is fine, because kids have an incredible way of forgiving themselves for the dozens upon dozens of white lies told to their parents.

If one of us really wanted a pet of some kind and begged long enough, eventually one of our parents capitulated. They were serious about the kid being responsible for the animal, to the point that it almost seemed a little cruel. *The cat hasn't been fed all day? Too bad, it's your pet and you're responsible and someone will get around to it. The dog needs to go out and has been standing by the door for twenty minutes? Not my job. Take care of your dog.*

Knowing full well that the environment was especially ripe for all sorts of big requests after the divorce, I begged for weeks for a teddy bear hamster. I knew exactly what I was doing. Kids are fantastic when it comes to subtle psychological manipulation. A company making cute plastic hamster habitats connected by a series of tubes and caps was advertising them over cartoon commercial breaks. No one really wanted rodents in the house, but I begged and begged and emerged victorious when on Christmas morning, I opened my bedroom door and there in all its glory was the hamster habitat with the cutest little teddy bear hamster you ever saw.

I was on cloud nine for days and sat and watched "Teddy" for hours over Christmas break. I set him loose in my dollhouse and watched him climb the stairs and walk over the tiny beds and knock over tables and chairs. I didn't know it at the time, but teddy bear hamsters are extremely common and not very expensive. Still, I felt I had scored big-time.

The problem with hamsters, other than the fact that they are not nearly as sweet or social as their cute little faces suggest, is that they are nocturnal, and so they're not very friendly or happy during the day. They really don't want anything to do with anyone during the day. They also bite. They can bite hard and even break the skin if you irritate them enough.

One warm summer day when I was holding "Teddy" in my second-floor room, he suddenly and without any warning bit my finger—hard—and I flinched. I also happened to be standing by an open bedroom window. Out he went. It was one of those moments in time where the air and movements were heavy and slow and I lunged my head out the window, expecting to see him flattened on the ground below or impaled in a nearby bush. Nothing. I looked and looked and was breathing so hard I thought I'd faint when I noticed the tiniest of two little hamster hands holding onto the very edge of the window sill. He survived! It was a miracle! I scooped him up in my hands and quickly put him back in his cage.

I don't remember him biting me after that. He either learned his lesson, or I was much less cavalier in holding him from that point forward.

177

Teddy also happened to be a she. We learned this when she went on to give birth to a tiny village of translucent baby hamsters. Not once did I hold one near an open window. With a new team of hamsters, they worked together and chewed and chewed through the plastic habitat caps, breaking out one late spring day when I decided to take them out for a bit of sunshine, briefly leaving them unattended. Only one hamster remained, spinning away on the hamster wheel, completely unaware of the great hamster escape. I was back to one hamster and this meant I was clearly ready to add another pet or two to my collection.

One Easter, our dad set up a bunny display at the country club. Not having any takers at the end of the day, he let us take the three bunnies home. So we tried rabbits for a while too. Well, why not? It didn't take long to have a few more bunnies show up and in captivity, they didn't do as well, but I was eleven or twelve years old in charge of small bunny breeding population. Without any Internet for guidance, I turned to the *Encyclopedia Britannica* set for help on how to take care of baby bunnies and their parents. I fed them and cleaned their pen and I knew full well that it was me who was in charge of them, although I am fairly certain I fell short in all sorts of ways.

Like security, for example. Rabbits, in neighborhoods where people don't think their hunting dog breeds can wander around without a leash, are at risk. This isn't something your average kid would come to realize unless things went drastically south—and they did.

One Saturday morning in early spring, I was sitting in our sunroom watching weekly cartoons when I heard something weird—dogs barking out in our yard. Crackers, our Basset Hound, was inside next to me, looking completely disinterested. I was about to turn back to the cartoons when it struck me. There were dogs in the rabbit pen. I ran out into the yard in my pajamas, no shoes, scrambling across the cold, wet grass, screaming and chased them off, which wasn't very smart at all. We never figured out just how and why a small pack of dogs was out roaming a residential neighborhood, but two of the three rabbits managed to escape.

A few days later, back at our miniature hobby farm, Morgan and I went out to clean up the remnants of the pen when he noticed a small piece of towel sticking out of the ground under a piece of plywood. He pulled on it, and out rolled nine fuzzy, and very alive, baby bunnies. My rabbit had hidden them as if she somehow knew of danger ahead, or had realized that her caretaker was woefully deficient in her security measures. We quickly took them indoors and for weeks, I bottle-fed them. Several actually survived.

Affirmations come in the strangest forms and suddenly, I fancied myself as sort of a junior veterinarian. An unlicensed one without medicine, but no one was watching, so technically it was pretty unlikely I'd be shut down by the Wisconsin Department of Natural Resources.

At some point, we stopped keeping track. Animals would just show up. There was a guinea pig no one seemed to have asked for or even wanted. For all we knew, he could have been dropped off by a friend or a neighbor. A parakeet flew out of the sky and onto Pat's shoulder. Another pet. A cat wandered into the yard, looking for food. Another pet. A carnival game involving ping-pong balls tossed into fishbowls and free goldfish. More pets.

There was just too much going on in our house but in all fairness, not a single one of us tried to pretend things were ever actually under control. What would have been the point?

"Waitress, You Slay!"

THERE WERE MANY MOUTHS TO feed and a thriving zoo back at home, so all the while, our mom was waitressing to help make extra money at a nearby diner by the name of "Round-the-Clock." The waitresses wore dark-brown uniforms with white blouses with ruffled collars and sleeves that made them look like some sort of Swiss schoolgirls. The uniforms included orange-tan-colored support pantyhose that came in plastic, silver-colored eggs we kids used for all sorts of crafts. The waitresses also wore the white support shoes you would expect to see in the healthcare industry.

True to its name, the diner was in fact open twenty-four hours a day, seven days a week. A large, bright neon sign hung out in front; the clock in it featured minute and hour hands that may have never moved. The Round-the-Clock was also one of those Greek-owned places that had an impossibly large menu, both in the actual size of the menu, which was laminated and about two feet high, and the food selection. The place offered endless menu choices and there seemed to be no rhyme nor reason to them. You could find everything from gyros to spaghetti to patty melts to chop suey to Denver omelets and Belgian waffles. I always thought adding a city or country to food made it more exotic, in a way.

The ingredients required to support such a wide array of dishes must have required its own small grocery store. Yet somehow, the Round-the-Clock never seemed short on anything. The place was never too busy and never too empty and was lined with booths with orange vinyl benches and light-brown Formica tables. Toward the kitchen stood a u-shaped counter with the kind of swivel chairs we kids loved to sit on, endlessly spinning in circles.

The diner was owned and run by a couple of brothers who spoke mostly Greek and enough English to run an American business. They knew how to cook, if short-order cooking counts. Their patrons came to eat after finishing second and third shifts at factories or other jobs, to have a cup of coffee and an inexpensive breakfast before heading home. They sat at the counter or a nearby booth, sporting old uniforms with name tags worn for so many years the men forgot they were even wearing them.

Our mom had made friends at work and so at least going to work wasn't so awful for her. One of her buddies was another waitress named Bonnie, who was funny, older and silly all at once—she was the kind of person you can't help but like and exactly what you would want in a waitress. Nothing seemed to bother her and she was perpetually upbeat.

Overall, the group of waitresses worked hard for tips in a town that was notoriously frugal, so they were at a bit of a disadvantage. They worked long shifts, day after day without expecting much out of life other than a way to pay for food, bills, and an occasional splurge at the flea market or a garage sale. These weren't women who were envious about others who had more. They didn't have time to worry about how their families compared to the ones with better-paying jobs. Life was busy and exhausting enough without those sorts of concerns. Like women in third-world countries lagging in equality and proper healthcare, they were too concerned about putting food on their family's plates to have the time or capacity to worry about anything else.

These women represented a large class of individuals who didn't know what they didn't know. They didn't have a lifeline of lawyers or health advocates or political representatives to somehow make life more fair for them. They were not in the company of professionals who found themselves in the company of other professionals, who whether they knew it or not, gave them a network of connections and huge advantages over the working class. These waitresses, like other working-class folks, had families to support. The plain reality is that opportunities presented to women working late nights at a diner aren't the same as men and women going to black-tie galas or fundraisers.

The knowledge gap is especially painful when you realize that the undereducated suffer heartache and loss, which could either be prevented or dealt with through legal or other channels. Racine wasn't known for its high-powered attorneys or headliner court cases. So when the twenty-something-year-old son of one waitress was arrested and landed in a jail in northern Wisconsin and died from "suicide," though he never ever had any signs of suicidal thoughts in the past, no one did anything about it. There was no lawyer, no call to a states' attorney, no visit to the local police to put pressure on them for an investigation.

The absence of social media meant there was no way to effectively mount a campaign against what the waitress and her family surely knew in their hearts to be a miscarriage of justice. The majority of working folk simply does not have the wherewithal to lawyer up. So on top of the pain of having lost a child, the parents suffered the extra turmoil of never really knowing what happened, never knowing if their child's death had been caused by the negligence or illegal actions of another. In other words, there could never be any closure.

Another waitress lost an adult daughter to cancer likely caused by jobsite exposures. Again, speculation and heartbreak, but no real answers.

These waitresses, to whom so many never even gave a second thought, had more strength and bravery just in having to deal with the things life threw at them than anyone could ever imagine. They represent the type of people who view grieving as a luxury rather than the necessary process that it actually is, because there is just no time to ponder or grieve. Bills had to be paid and so this small group of waitresses carried on, refilling ketchup bottles and salt shakers day after day, making friends, crying, laughing, and finding contentment in the little things in life.

All the while, it seems that Jackie, our mom, was silently mounting sweet revenge against the man who had left her after six kids and 23 years of marriage. As a waitress at Round-the-Clock, she no doubt had some down time and eventually set her eyes on one of the line cooks, who was fifteen years her junior.

Leonidas, a/k/a Lee, was nearly fresh off the boat from Greece. He was small in stature and had a handlebar mustache, which may or may not have made him look more American, if that is what he was hoping to achieve. On weekends, he played in a men's soccer league with his Greek friends. He didn't drink or use drugs, and was a decent guy and acceptable on most fronts but for the age thing, which put him just a few years older than our brother Tim. Our family, in particular our mom, found a way to make the age difference more acceptable by focusing on Lee's maturity level, rather than his chronological age alone.

Our mom and Lee started seeing each other regularly and having spent most of her last two decades raising kids, this was finally her time. Along with her newfound dating freedom, our

` mom laughed and had more fun than we had seen her have in a very long time.

It was around this time that she clearly decided to take matters into her own hands and make a change and take control of her appearance, which had sat solidly on the backburner of her life for the past decade while she was treading water taking care of kids and a philandering husband. She had never really bought clothes or things for herself, and certainly had little spare time to even think of doing so. When she wasn't cleaning or cooking, she spent most of her time trying to keep up with a husband who was quickly slipping through her fingers. Our mom decided to approach her forties, as well as the natural aging process, like a lion fighting off a hyena.

Our mom took a steady dose of—from my view—a magical mix of Jane Fonda workout videos, Dexatrim diet pills, and SlimFast shakes, which at the time were all the rage. She sat out on the small concrete slab behind our townhome, tanning herself to look even thinner. She seemed to get a little blonder and if she did do anything with her hair, it was strictly color "out of a box." Once a month or so, she would put on a pair of thin plastic gloves, mix a purplish-looking solution that smelled as though it had nothing short of an industrial bleach in it, and put it on her short hair, which she also cut herself. Jackie was practical and self-sufficient to the core, all while being remarkably economical.

She spent many of her days and nights at work and so she made new friends with the other waitresses, some much younger. These were the driving force in the group heading to the local version of Studio 54 to go dancing. Mom amassed a collection of eight-track tapes featuring anyone from Donna Summer to Pablo Cruise to pianists Ferrante and Teicher, and some of us kids became just a little obsessed with pulling eight-track tapes in and out of the player, from one musical genre to the next, when no one was around.

One day, our mom announced her twenty-fifth year high school reunion was coming, and "Come hell or high water, I'm going!" She was no doubt excited to show off her new look and took me shopping with her at the mall to help her pick out the appropriate high-school-reunion revenge outfit. She went with Gloria Vanderbilt jeans, a little tight but not too tight, cute boots, and a white blouse. She looked great. It was well worth the splurge. As for the reunion, she opted against bringing a date, although I secretly hoped she would bring her much younger, foreign boyfriend just to get a rise out of her classmates.

The Greeks

WE DIDN'T KNOW IT AT THE TIME, but the relationship with our mom's Greek boyfriend indirectly helped us keep the house on Northwestern Avenue a few more years. Lee seemed to like hanging around people older than him. He had a large group of Greek friends in their fifties and sixties who enjoyed playing poker on the weekends. They needed a place to have their poker games and were willing to pay a host, since apparently their wives weren't too keen on having them play at home.

Thus began the "Poker Players" era. Every Friday and Saturday night, a group of ten to fifteen Greeks parked their cars on the street adjacent to our house, and let themselves in through the back door around 8 p.m. There would be a basic set up of two large percolators of coffee, with a service of cream, sugar and Styrofoam cups, as well as some deli sandwiches

192

on white bread. Nothing too expensive, nothing too fancy. After all, poker was the focus, with less attention placed on the gambling aspect. A large pile of single dollar bills accumulated in the middle of the table, but knowing this group, it could not have been a lot of money.

The poker games continued until way past my junior high school bedtime, sometimes lasting until two or three in the morning. The guys played in our dining room, which was set back a bit from the rest of the house; we were largely able to avoid any interaction with them. If we happened to be in the sunroom-turned-family room a few rooms over, it was easy to pick up on and learn Greek curse words, because they were typically the loudest and were repeated many, many times.

The mornings after, in exchange for payment of a dollar or two, I happily cleaned out the ashtrays because I also learned that this activity presented a sought-after opportunity to find and repair a few extra bucks in the form of torn-up dollar bills. One of the poker players, after losing a hand, would tear up a dollar bill or two in anger, shredding the money into tiny pieces, and leaving these on one of the trays set up at each corner of the dining table. It only took a bit of tape and patience, and *voilá*, more money. To me, it felt like a visit from the Tooth Fairy.

The poker players kept coming back, week after week, for months or years. They did so to have the privilege of playing poker in our home, uninterrupted, no wives or kids, smoking cigarettes and drinking coffee all night long. Not one of them drank alcohol or was rude to our mom, ever. The best part, of course, was that they paid her handsomely from the gambling proceeds for the room rental. By then, with an ex-husband out of another job and Mom out of work with late mortgage payments and literally no child support, it was as if someone had thrown us a lifeline to prevent the foreclosure on the house we all had come to love.

The long line of parked cars every Friday and Saturday did not go unnoticed by the neighborhood, though. I often had volleyball, cheerleading, or some activity that ran past dinner. I don't recall walking home alone in the dark because even a family like mine had limits. I'd either wait to be the last to get picked up by one of my older siblings, or I'd get a ride home with my classmate Annie Johnson's mom, bless her heart, because our house was on their way home.

Each time she dropped me off, on noticing the cars, Mrs. Johnson, who was a bit of a busybody, would ask, "So, Kathleen, is your mom having a party or something?" Or she might change up the question in hope of actually getting a direct response: "Kathleen, is there something going on at your house?" Of course, any pre-teen or teenager with half a brain—like me—knew well enough not to upset the apple cart and keep things in play. Moreover, we needed to keep the money coming to pay the bills and it was thus imperative that I kept my mouth shut. My reply was without fail both vague and im- mensely frustrating to the meddling

Mrs. Johnson: "No, nothing, really, I don't know." I thought I was doing a great job keeping her at bay.

Eventually, the gig was up and someone must have reported the clandestine games to the police. It was either a pissed-off wife or Mrs. Johnson or even our dad, for that matter. We never did learn the true identity of the snitch.

The night it all went down was one for the ages. I was sitting on the living room floor with my mom, going through and sorting old spools of sewing thread, when at least six of Racine's finest busted through our side door in full force, bullet-proof vests and all, as though some dark, nefarious activity lay in wait for them beyond the rickety side screen door.

The officers marched through the family room, into the living room, and then into the dining room, busting up what must have been in their minds the most exciting criminal enterprise on the north side of Racine.

Surely they had to realize when they approached the poker table that it was a group of old friends? Even though it had to be readily apparent that they wrongly assessed the situation, the officers maintained a look of sheer determination as they shouted orders at the poker players, demanding them to comply. It turned out that "Officer Friendly," the sweet man who visited our grade school over the years, teaching us not to be afraid of our helpful police officers, wasn't so damned friendly after all.

Soon after the raid, out marched the perpetrators with the police, in handcuffs and all. It was quite a show. As the players made their way past our mom, she was understandably taken aback and was totally shocked by it all. It certainly didn't help when she blurted out an extraordinarily self-incriminating "Uh-oh!" which seemed misplaced and inappropriate on so many levels. First, she knew she was in no position to defend herself or make any sort of statement whatsoever. Second, she had been sitting around with her twelve-year-old daughter when it happened and so it just looked bad.

Third, the whole mess would have been avoidable had she simply properly locked the side door.

At some point, these police officers had to accept that what they had encountered was just a small-time poker game among a group of harmless immigrant friends. No drinking, no drugs, not even a lot of money being gambled, for that matter. If the men in blue found any of it the least bit exciting, they had to have been facing an incredibly slow period when it came to crime in the city.

Apparently, the state's attorney was over-zealous and bored too, because he prosecuted our mom for having a disorderly household and the poker players for some form of criminal gambling amongst friends. The raid had to be justified, of course. In the end, there was no jail time, a few fines, and a reduced fine for a little old man by the name of Carl, who was collecting his pension by this time and so the judge didn't have it in him to punish an elderly man.

The funny part about the poker-player bust is the fact that the Racine police missed what would have likely been something that would have been much more interesting to the Racine State's Attorney. One floor above the dining room where the poker players sat was the hidden crawl space behind a long, narrow closet, where my brother John was growing a respectable amount of weed with the help of ultra-violet lights and seeds from friends. The old house was designed with so many odd nooks and crannies and corners and it had to have been useful during Prohibition. Clearly the drugs growing just above the cops' heads would have brought about a higher level of respect amongst the ranks of the Racine Police Department.

When we lost the poker players, we lost the house. Not the same day, of course, but it seemed things moved quickly after that. The police weren't exactly empowered to return the next morning with a moving van and a dictate of: "O.K., kids, time to get out!" But we lost the house soon after.

The money from the poker kitty had had a remarkable way of keeping us above water for some time. Whether because of the poor economy or lack of effort or some combination thereof, our dad was still out of work and there was no way a waitress's wages from a twenty-four hour diner would meet mortgage payments and other bills.

Our mom was able to stave off the inevitable for a short period of time, making ends meet by applying for Public Aid. It didn't make sense. We lived in a big house but we were barely holding on and people in the community who had any idea that we were on welfare, using food stamps to buy food, must have thought we were a bunch of conniving frauds.

If anything, the entire experience was a lesson to all of us. Don't judge. You have no idea what another family is going through or how they got there. They might just be barely hanging on to whatever they have, though no fault of their own.

The house was on the market for what seemed like years. No one wanted to buy it or no one could afford it. Maybe it was just in a weird spot on a somewhat busy street next to a funeral home. Not a single penny had been put into the upkeep of the home, because there wasn't a single penny to spare. The proximity to a funeral home never bothered us, nor did the busy street, but the house barely got a showing.

We found ourselves in the odd predicament in that we couldn't afford the house, but we couldn't find a way to get out and live somewhere else, either. We were living in the 1980s before the age of blaming others for overextended mortgages and loan forgiveness and the media making mortgage companies the bad guys. *You can't afford it? You can't make your payments? Tough luck, you're out.*

The bank gave us some time but eventually things caught up and out we went. Thankfully, most of us managed to escape serious injury, staying relatively healthy, at a time when there was no hope of health insurance on a waitress salary.

Irresponsibly, we clung to the fleeting notion of keeping the house in the face of months of missed mortgage payments. Our mom did everything she could to make ends meet, surplus dairy, handouts, whatever it took. I'd go with my mom to the grocery store and felt the flush of shame when it came time to check out and she pulled out the food stamps. It had to have been miserable and embarrassing for her, and I probably managed to make it worse.

Some days, I'd stare right back at the others in line, angry at the obvious looks of judgment on their faces. Other times, I would stand off to the side, just enough away from her to make an invisible fence between us, looking away, distancing myself from all of it, pretending that I wasn't really part of it all. We could have all done a better job at supporting her, but kids don't always do their best.

Georgetown–
But Not THAT Georgetown

FINALLY, FORECLOSURE CAME AND we were forced to move. There wasn't a lot of thinking about it, talking about it, or crying about it. Blaming the bank or government for failed mortgages was not yet a thing and even if it had been, it would have been very unlike anyone in our family to officially take up a charge against anyone in power. The adult members of our family—namely our parents— either didn't feel qualified or righteous enough to doubt those in positions that were over ours, whether socially or economically. Instead, we harbored a steady amount of ill will against the institutions and those working for them. Mostly though, we accepted our consequences and found a way to move on.

Racine, like much of the Badger State, is a hodgepodge of cultures and people and religions and races, with pockets of cultural groups living in neighborhoods all over town. Through the decades, residents were distributed due to a variety of related factors, including schools and expenses, but most of all, jobs. Main Street in downtown Racine appears to be where everything started, with a combination of charming old storefronts, sprinkled with a few deserted businesses. The easternmost part of Racine is bordered by Lake Michigan and a surprisingly expansive and sandy beach known as North Beach Park. Like the rest of the town, the beaches are remarkably underrated with immeasurable potential. The western part of Racine County, consisting of acres and acres of farm fields, is remote, like the farmers in charge of them.

Brother Pat returned from Illinois again and so he, Morgan, me, and our mom moved to a different neighborhood on the other side of town, in the southern part of the county. It was an area with newer, less expensive, less interesting developments created by builders focused on money, not aesthetics.

Sam the Great Dane had never been neutered, so he made a game of escaping the yard and impregnating little bitches all over town while he lived with us. Before we moved, Sam had already been sent to a farm. Not the sort of dog farm of lore where the dogs don't actually come back, because they didn't actually end up on a farm, now did they? But an actual farm in western Racine County, where he would live out his remaining years as the best big dog he could be.

After Sam, we had opted for a more sedentary dog, a Bassett Hound named Crackers from a shelter. He didn't do much of anything but beg, bark at people, and look sad, mostly to get more food. Above all, he was really, really good at begging. Just before the move, he went to another home with younger kids more interested in him and gave him a better life. He was just there one day and gone the next. Truth be told and fortunately so, kids in junior and high school are so completely immersed in their own tiny universes that the rest of the world momentarily dissolves around them. Re-homing a pet was sad, certainly, but not as tragic as it could be under more normal circumstances.

We ended up renting a townhome that was nearly identical to the dozens and dozens of other townhomes found on the newly developed South Side. There was a bit of brick with the majority consisting of aluminum siding, small bedrooms, small kitchen, small living room, all made possible by less expensive construction. There were minor variations in the patterns and colors of the siding and brick, which was a weak effort to make them look more interesting. We hoped our time in the new home wouldn't last long. However, we ended up spending the next five years in the Georgetown neighborhood.

Much like the fact that 2932 Northwestern Avenue had nothing to do with Northwestern University, Georgetown had absolutely no relationship to any East Coast institution of higher learning. The decision to call the neighborhood "Georgetown" most certainly involved someone with no clue about Georgetown University. It was more probable that the area was named by some guy named George or by someone with a really poor sense of humor.

Our Georgetown was a lower-income development with small ranch-style homes, multi-unit rentals, and apartment complexes. There was a sign somewhere at one of the entrances to the area confirming it was indeed named Georgetown. Nothing university, East Coast, or even George-like or Georgian about it.

The whole process of moving again, under much less promising circumstances, could not have been easy for our mom, not even for a second. Kids are different, though. At least, we were. Our focus was on friends and school; spending time at home was not a major priority. Nor was there a lot of drama or dwelling on the sudden change; if we did get dramatic, it really didn't get you very far in our family. It turns out the same is often true in life.

The upside of renting a townhome was that there would no longer be the feel of an old, drafty house with poorly functioning plumbing and appliances. The townhouse was smaller and so turning up the thermostat actually meant the place would get warmer. We loved that. Plus, for the first time in our lives, we had the luxury of central air. It was cold in every single room when we really needed it and sometimes, on terribly hot summer days, we were allowed to close the windows and turn on the air conditioning full blast.

Everything in the townhome, like dozens of others in the neighborhood, was on the newer side. It wasn't our home or even our appliances, but it all seemed on the new side, not like the old ones we had moved away from, so that was good. We weren't the family in the interesting old home on the block any longer. We mixed in with everyone else and the other Georgetown kids treated us like one of them and that was perfectly fine.

Years later, driving through the neighborhood with my husband and children on a trip
down memory lane, one of them commented
that the townhomes, now a bit dated and
somewhat worse for the wear, looked "sad." At
first I agreed, but then it immediately occurred
to me I was dead wrong. I remembered that as a
family, we were generally happy in that townhome. There may have been more worries than
money, but there certainly was no shortage of
laughter, family, and friends. I reminded my
children that you can never, ever really know the
happiness of the people inside a home by
looking at its exterior and making assumptions
like that is just a mistake.

At the entrance of the Georgetown neighborhood sat a small shopping center, home to a
convenience store, a gas station, a few commercial office spaces for a few unrelated small
businesses, and a pizza place named Ferraro's
that had no dining room. Delivery or takeout
only, nothing fancy. On Wednesdays, they had a
fried chicken special, which, if you had a really,

really good week, you'd have that meal for dinner. Kids walked home from Ferraro's proudly displaying Styrofoam containers.

Most kids were free to roam the neighborhood and overall, it was a good place to meet friends of varying racial but similar economic backgrounds. Their parents either worked all the time or were nowhere to be found for other reasons. We were part of a group of uber-independent kids with the only real curfew to worry about was the one imposed by the City of Racine. Each night, an announcement came on the T.V.: "It's 10 p.m. Parents, do you know where your children are?"

It also happened to be the same neighborhood where Lee's parents lived. Of all the places we moved to, it was precisely one-third of a block away from our mother's younger boyfriend. Clever one, Jackie.

The new neighborhood was too far away from Sacred Heart School, which meant that we had to switch to Racine's public school system.

My school was Mitchell Junior High School and kids from Georgetown took the bus.

Mom's boyfriend Lee had a much younger sister named Helen, who was fun and funny and goofy; I liked her immediately. I infiltrated the family and learned a few Greek words. Lee's parents really liked me, even if it wasn't quite clear they had actually accepted the much older, new girlfriend to their middle son, who also happened to be my mom. Lee's sister Helen sang in the choir and I joined too, along with the other kids who weren't very good at other things like sports.

For whatever reason, I got it into my head that I would attend a year of Greek School at Helen's church. For anyone familiar with the culture, this isn't the sort of thing that non-Greek kids normally do. Usually, it's a way for Greek parents to force heavy doses of everything Greek on their American-born children, to make sure their kids stay true to the culture. If things work out the way they are supposed to, the kids would meet and eventually marry another Greek and on and on it goes.

I was clearly the outsider while I studied and learned the Greek alphabet and started speaking and writing Greek and learned a culture which had absolutely nothing to do with my own. At the age of thirteen, with no background in the language whatsoever, I was placed in the language class that started with little kids in little chairs until they figured out this was ridiculous. Even a non-Greek can learn the language quickly. Thankfully, they soon moved me up to a table with older kids where I didn't have to hunch over to read and write.

There were little Greek dances and songs and each week it was like a visit to the Greek Isles, except that it all took place in the hall of a Greek Orthodox Church in Wisconsin. At the end of the first year, there was a "graduation" party, which meant we each had to stand up in front of a bunch of Greek people and recite a poem. I was petrified when it came to public speaking at that point, but for whatever reason, I wasn't worried at all. Mom even bought me a new dress and let a friend perm my hair.

It was a different language and I was an outsider, so I assumed expectations were pretty low from the audience of Greeks. As it turns out, I nailed it. In fact, to this day, I can still recite the first line of a Greek poem about some Greek flower. And then, the whole school thing was over and all the Greek families stood around eating Greek food and I realized I really had no business in this whole Greek thing anyway.

Mitchell Junior High was like entering a medieval fortress. Large, dark, smelly, and filled with people who were really tough, or who did a great job acting as though they were. Kids were careful to watch their mouths because if you crossed someone just so, there was the distinct possibility of facing retribution in the form of a tap, a shove, or a punch. There wasn't much thought to doing anything about it, after all justice was swift and unquestionable. Without cameras in the halls or outside the schools, there was zero concern about getting caught.

Kids like me who thought they had mastered the ability to be invisible soon learned it no longer worked, especially in gym class. This was especially hard on the girls. Following each gym class, students were required to do the "walk" through the long shower corridor, completely naked, towel over the head, while the short, stout, no-nonsense former semi-professional softball player turned gym teacher checked kids off as having both showered, and most definitely humiliated. It was something we never got used to and dreaded with every ounce of the spirit each and every time. As if going through puberty wasn't bad enough, try walking through the smelly showers of an old public-school gym with nothing but a towel slightly larger than a washcloth as your only defense.

After a few weeks of school, either the choir director or the other kids decided the name Kathleen was too odd or too hard to pronounce, and so my name momentarily morphed from

Kathleen to Kathy. To be specific, it was not Kathy with a "y", but Kathi with an "i." And the "i' was not dotted, but had a heart over it, because these are the things that foolish and immature junior high school girls do, all the time. The name change was quickly put to the test when friends started calling our home, asking for a girl named Kathi, with a heart over the "i."

Pat and Morgan found this highly entertaining and just added to a long list of reasons to make fun of me for the idiotic things I apparently did on a daily basis. Our mom was not so entertained. My name was to be Kathleen and that was it. No nicknames allowed. After a few calls in which she was clearly frustrated by the mention of "Kathi," she started a new approach, telling the caller, while standing in front of me, that they had the right number and waited while the person on the other line eventually hung up the phone.

Pat and Morgan stood nearby, grinning ear to ear. This went on for a while until finally the caller figured it out—or I explained to them at school—that my mother was a lunatic obsessed for no apparent reason with the name Kathleen.

Our mom's odd fixation with controlling what others would call me was a bit of an exception. She, like other parents in our neighborhood, was at the opposite end of the continuum compared to modern "helicopter" parents. As a result, in the Georgetown neighborhood, unsupervised activities abounded, which not surprisingly went south at times. We experienced petty crimes and recreational drugs and guns in homes that should not have had them. Morgan found a group of new friends in the neighborhood who were generally nice kids, but ended up changing his trajectory.

Without a lot to do, without a lot of money, and without a meddling parent standing by, creating activities and opportunities, kids will find ways to entertain themselves. To many young people who wandered the neighborhood and did whatever they pleased, getting high and drinking booze as early as the eighth grade in Georgetown was not unusual. That went on into high school. When I was in college, it became abundantly clear to me that most kids didn't grow up like the ones from Georgetown, having developed a decent tolerance for booze.

One day, thankfully a time when Morgan wasn't with his new companions, one of them picked up a gun and accidentally shot one of the other boys in the group. How and why the gun materialized was never really known, but it wasn't an occurrence very novel or unique in Georgetown. Guns were around, not talked about much, not really a worry in any obvious way, but they were there and unfortunately, teenage kids without enough to do found their way to all of them.

The poor kid's last words were: "Jimmy, you shot me, you fucker." He was right. Jimmy was a little fucker, but no one ever believed he was the type of fucker who would do anything beyond negligent. Most of all, Jimmy certainly was not the type of kid who should be shouldered with handling the guilt of an accidental shooting for the rest of his life. He didn't possess enough of a thought in his mind to do anything intentionally, because most Georgetown kids had no interest or thought about the future ahead of them.

Other friendships from our old neighborhood remained intact despite our move. Somehow, there were unexplained pockets of friends who met terrible fates. One had an aneurysm, another a heart attack, and a boy named Matt Leskowitz lost control of his car in front of our first home, hitting the very mailbox that seemed to get mowed down each winter by an errant car. He went on to strike a nearby telephone pole and was killed instantly. The series of random unrelated events in a small circle of friends left the few remaining ones a little broken in one way or another.

Tractor Company High School

A DECISION WAS MADE BY SOMEONE, somewhere within the Racine Unified School District, that a high school built on the far west side of town close to the farming areas would closely resemble a Soviet prison. Large, tan, and block-like in appearance, with a few tiny windows here and there, that high school maintained this look over the years. It was as though zoning either didn't exist at the time the school design was approved, or zoning was run by a small group of schizophrenic urban planners.

Another decision was made to name this reformatory-like structure after a large tractor manufacturer in town. J.I. Case High School was placed out in the boonies near farm fields and an ever-growing and imposing landfill. In this case, "landfill" was a bit of a misnomer. Land wasn't being filled at all; in fact, garbage was continuously dumped week after week until it reached an astonishing height during our tenure at J.I. Case. The stench from the landfill was unsurprisingly terrible.

The school colors were green and gold like those of the Green Bay Packers and so most of us felt pretty good about that. Students were bused in from all parts of Racine as a way to integrate kids from different areas and different colors. In the Georgetown neighborhood, that integration was already there. The Georgetown bus was a mix of white, black, and brown. Never for a second did any of us believe there was anything unusual or noteworthy about it. The busing program meant that farm kids, urban kids, and suburban kids of as many colors and more were educated under a single cinder-block roof.

Case was run by a principal by the name of Mr. Mitchell. He was tall, thin, had a mustache, and what looked like the start of an Afro that he never got around to finishing. Without fail, he sported an impressive three-piece suit. Everyone loved him. We mostly saw him roaming the cafeteria at lunch time. He always seemed to be running a positive public relations campaign on behalf of the entire school administration.

Mr. Mitchell, from outward appearances, was always friendly, smiling, and approachable in a way that most other teachers were not. He was good for a high-five or a handshake or just a general hello. As students, we had no idea if he was actually listening to anything we had to say, but he was amiable and kind-spirited in a way that most school bosses seem to lose over the years.

Kids who got into trouble may have known Mr. Mitchell a bit better than the ones who didn't, but there wasn't any animosity or hard feelings. If you got detention for smoking cigarettes or pot or for fighting, you'd stay after school. If it happened a lot, like it did with my brother Morgan, you ended up in classrooms outside the school set up in construction trailers. None of us ever knew exactly why, or whether this was planned, or if they just wanted to keep the "bad" kids out of the general population like solitary confinement.

Most high school kids weren't in the business of questioning things that might put them above the radar, open to criticism, ridicule or worse, arbitrary punishment. There were guards in the hallways to keep fights to a minimum. In addition, there were gangs and there were drugs. The school also had its groups of athletes and honor-roll-type kids who were good about avoiding trouble.

With the great range of kids and backgrounds, parties ran the gamut. There were barn parties and parties out on a prairie to "house parties" on Martin Luther King Drive where you had to pay an entry fee to an older brother or parent for a red solo cup before you got in. After one house party hosted by a friend, our small clique decided it was way too crowded, the ceiling way too low, and the house far too much of a fire hazard for even our mildly developed teenage brains to accept. We left early, walked over to our car nearby, and were rewarded for what we considered good judgment when a group of younger teenage kids with knives ripped the purses off our shoulders. This wasn't something so shocking or unusual but we pleaded for the return of the non-monetary items in our purses, which was a reasonable enough request. Believe it or not, the transaction ended with one of the kids tossing a few of our worthless items back to us.

At some point, I ended up in mostly advanced placement classes and so my group of friends shifted to the kids in those classes. They weren't Georgetown kids. They came from bigger homes, from traditional families with parents who had money to afford gymnastics, dance, and art classes, along with the time and energy to attend their kids' sports events. I was a shameless opportunist and found a way to make our meager Georgetown home the center of activity. There was a revolving door of friends and parties week after week while our mom waitressed late hours Friday and Saturday nights at an Italian restaurant named Infusino's.

Infusino's had been started by three brothers from southern Italy. The general opinion of
the staff was one brother was small and sweet,
one was overweight and a bit of a bully, and the
third was thin and shrewd. The place became
one of the most popular restaurants in town,
known for large quantities of Italian food and
above all, cheapish prices. Weekends meant
people lined up out the door so as a waitress,
our mom had hit the gold mine in tips. It was as
good as she could do.

With the head of the household out working
most weekend nights, our group of high school
friends had the unique opportunity to have a
place to drink, uninterrupted. It was unlucky or
lucky, depending on the perspective. We could
safely remain in a little drunken social bubble,
drinking everything we could get our hands on,
from cheap beer to vodka to pink "champagne"
that had nothing to do with the small area in
France where real champagne is cultivated. Once
everyone left, we did a meticulous clean-up of

the entire house—which didn't take long at all—
followed by the disposal of any evidence.

Pat and Morgan were never, ever around, so
my small group of high-performing student-
drinker friends had the place to themselves.
Aside from consuming copious amounts of
alcohol, in retrospect, we were remarkably well-
behaved and looked out for one another. We had
goals and plans beyond high school and so we
knew that we needed to keep whatever level of
misbehavior we engaged in within a manageable
range.

If a high school student was serious about
making his or her life any better, it meant
studying and studying and preparing for the
SATs. The morning of the SAT exams, I got up,
made myself breakfast, and was about to head
out the door to drive myself to the SAT exam in
one of our long line of jalopy cars. Mom came
into the kitchen and told me very matter-of-
factly: "You're on your own when it comes to
college. I don't know a thing about it, and I can't
help you."

Neither of us had a clue about the secret world of tutoring, test prep classes, and SAT camps held for wealthy high school kids over the weekend at Ivy League schools. Nor did we have a clue about the world of universities, colleges, applications, or exams. We weren't part of that world. It was alien to us and for all practical purposes, ignorance meant my own refusal to give up.

Though Tim and Margie were long gone from the Badger State, graduating high school, starting careers much more interesting than mine would ever be, John and Pat never seemed to make it out of high school. This was not based on a shortage of intelligence or talent, or even just raw skills or likeability. It was more likely due to a shortage of discipline and way too much free time and the ability to make money quickly at jobs closer to what our dad did in the restaurant industry.

At some point, each brother bounced around from one school to the next, all while holding jobs, and ultimately being sent to the "alternative" high school in Racine, Walden. It was widely recognized as a school of last resort and the final stop before dropping out entirely. Kids who had overworked, exhausted parents just weren't as likely to do as well. Without sports or some other legitimate activity to keep them moving toward a goal, they wandered. And there were a lot of things to wander toward: girls, drinking, weed, hanging out with other friends who didn't care too much about school, either. The kids who went to Walden really didn't give a shit what anyone thought, so for those on the outside looking in, judging, viewing the Walden kids as losers, well, that was just a colossal waste of time. Those kids simply didn't care.

Although it came as no surprise or disappointment to any of her children, our mom's relationship with Lee didn't work out. Even though time and time again, she was either physically or emotionally unavailable for me, I didn't want to see her hurt. She was heartbroken and cried loudly and without any restraint, in a way I'd never heard before, burying her face and endless tears in a towel. A towel, because a Kleenex would never have been be enough.

Our mom sat there at the little table barely lit up by a stained-glass lamp from the days at our old home, in our tiny kitchen, and sobbed and sobbed. It scared me because her crying jag lasted longer than anything I thought a person could endure. I discovered that I was an awful consoler. I was a teenage girl, which meant I was basically useless when it came to doing anything meaningful or impactful for adults.

Then our mom went to bed, slept, got up, and started her life all over again. Each day was a new beginning and the difference I know now and appreciate about her, just struggling to make ends meet for her family, provided her with resilience and mental toughness. Every day, she had to deal with a whole world of problems others don't think about. *Is my car going to actually make it to work this time? What will I do if my kids get sick if I don't have insurance? How in the hell am I going to pay all those bills on time this month?* She was barely keeping up. There was never any time or a way to get ahead.

It took college and a law degree before I realized how truly disadvantaged working-class people are —they don't know what they don't know. They don't presume to have rights and accept things that come their way, even when they are wrong and unfair. They don't stand up for themselves because they don't even know what or who there is to stand up to, and, barring someone else in the world coming to their rescue to help guide them through, they are and will be forever lost. That is, unless they happen to have a family member who decides to become a lawyer and goes on to practice law.

The Fourth of Racine

IT TAKES FOUR YEARS TO LEARN how to be a high school kid. Three years of posturing, pretending, hiding from bullies, and being anything but your real self. Finally, senior year comes around and things falls into place. High school kids start to let their guard down and realize they like each other, who also happen to be the same people they were freshman year.

Senior year is built around events only the graduating class really appreciates. The Racine prom is the closest thing to Hollywood the town will ever see. The high schools, which mostly hated each other the rest of the year, come together for a city-wide prom to end all proms. Seven high schools in total: three public high schools, one alternative high school, a Lutheran high school, a Catholic high school, and for the few that have extra money for a pricey private high school, one of those as well.

Smaller dances start at the respective schools until the time comes for the big dance. The motorcade heads from each school towards Memorial Hall downtown on the lakefront. Couples and groups of couples collaborate to come up with the most creative or noticeable transportation to get to the city-wide prom downtown. Parents, friends, and complete strangers line the streets for blocks and blocks to wave and cheer at the motorcade of limos, vintage cars, truck, tractors and anything the seniors could get their hands on to be in the motorcade, which in our year, included an elephant. Kids rent rooms without parental permission and have side parties at nearby hotels. The underage partying continues through the next day and the final summer for the graduating seniors begins.

Then, summer starts in full force. For weeks, the upcoming Fourth of July consumes the attention of the entire town for a day that consistently turns out to be a display of Americana at its finest. The whole town—the whole mixed and unmixed town—plans every second of the day around the nearly four-hour parade down Main Street, followed by nearby barbeques and fireworks on the lake.

Little kids, high school kids, sons and daughters home from college for the summer, and everyone up to little old ladies in their 90s line the street, saving spots overnight along the parade route with old blankets and lawn chairs. The day is part of the cultural fabric of the town; it will never, ever go away.

Absent any critique of the float-approval committee—if there is one—the range in the float quality is obvious and dramatic. Some floats clearly show a lot of time, thought, and effort went into them, like the "bronze soldiers" of Iwo Jima and the Vietnam War, painted head to toe in bronze, standing perfectly still for hours while holding an American flag. The crowd goes wild for them. Patriotism and the Fourth of July in a Midwestern town. No wonder the parade is crawling with politicians from the entire state.

Floats with Girl Scouts, local politicians, high school cheerleaders, and marching bands are kicked off by a fleet of fire trucks blaring their sirens, announcing the start of the parade. Floats with bands playing soul, country, heavy metal, and oldies music dot the lineup.

For me, the most Americana thing about the day is the assortment of people. Every color and shade and race are represented in the parade and in its spectators. Babies and small children of all combinations of skin colors wear red, white, and blue, waving flags, and throwing hand-held snap firecrackers on the ground.

One year, Mom was invited to a Fourth of July party at a home across from North Beach Park and had an incredible view of Lake Michigan. This particular Fourth of July party was hosted by a divorced dad of two by the name of Gerald Getzin. He went by Jerry and worked as a machinist at a plant in Milwaukee that made some of the largest mining machines in the world. He had blue eyes light as water that were kind, even if a bit judgmental on occasion. He was of German descent and had grown up on a farm that was eventually taken over by the City of Milwaukee when it came time to build a respectable airport. The farm was moved to Racine County west of the Interstate.

Jerry was simple but smart and tough in some ways, while kind in others. He looked at the world in a way that made everything seem a lot less complicated. Like our mom, he was Midwestern through and through, and didn't fall apart in the middle of a dreary, cold winter with no sign of the sun for weeks.

Over time, Jackie and Jerry decided they liked one another more than they liked being alone, and they moved in together. Eventually, they were married in the front room of the house overlooking Lake Michigan on a chilly but clear November day.

Through the high school years, college and law school, Jerry was a father figure I had always wanted without realizing the need was in there, and in me, he found another chance to be a better dad.

I'd come home visiting on holidays or a weekend and we'd get dinner at a tiny family restaurant nearby called Cliff's Boathouse, and enjoy Friday night fish fry in one of the quaintest little restaurants that felt like eating in a friend's kitchen. He listened while I unloaded all my worries and problems that to me, seemed impossible to overcome. Jerry always had a way of simplifying things in a way that only a former farmer could do and made me feel like everything would work out just fine. He was there for my college graduation and in pictures, he looked as proud to be there as any dad would be. Jerry represented the people who come into your life in ways the least expected.

* * *

Years later, after many years of dementia, he finally had to leave his home with its beautiful view of Lake Michigan sunrises, but at that point he wasn't even sure he left so there was the bright side of it. I went to visit him in a nursing home. He was in a wheelchair by then and although Mom did all she could to take care of him for years and years, it was just too much for her.

It was a bright spring day in April, the kind of day when the sun shone much too brightly with a temperature that was much too cold to make any sense. The flowers were beginning to bloom and the trees were starting to bud. The three of us sat for a while, looking at dozens of parakeets in a large aviary that took up the center of the first floor. We sat together not saying much at all, really. Eventually, I had to leave and so I wheeled Jerry back towards his room.

He hadn't communicated more than a few basic pleasantries that day, but when I left, I told him: "I love you, Jerry." It was something I'd certainly felt yet never told him before, but I knew it was time. He responded, clear as day: "I love you, too." We never got the chance to talk again after that, but in a way, the good-bye was perfectly Jerry.

True to the practical nature of a Wisconsin-ite, the memorial service was planned for a

Sunday so that friends and family wouldn't have to miss a single day's work. The only issue was that this particular date happened to fall on Mother's Day and so with three children in tow, I stood up in front of group of people and gave my step-father's eulogy on a Mother's Day I would surely never forget.

Badger Out

FINALLY, HIGH SCHOOL WAS OVER and it was time to move on. That's all I knew. I wanted to be away. As an eighteen-year-old girl, this translated into moving to another state, while the majority of my friends decided to go to the University of Wisconsin–Madison. I wanted to distance myself from this place, whether for a short time or forever. It could have been the place, the people, the memories, my family, or just wanting to be a part of something where I would always belong. It was likely a combination of all of those things.

This was an opportunity to leave the Badger State. My family had only lived here for ten years, but it seemed like a very long time. For kids, time takes forever. Days and weeks are long unless you're talking about summer vacation, which is never long enough. Kids with shorter timelines and fewer points of reference

238

really do have a point about things "taking forever." When you're older with a much longer path behind you, the hours, days, and years begin to fly by.

The drive to Saint Mary's College in South Bend, Indiana, was just over three hours from home, down a long toll road with a few indistinguishable farms and toll plazas. Mom, Jerry, and I drove down the beautiful tree-lined entrance to the college. We unpacked and set up my room; Jackie and Jerry left very unceremoniously with a brief goodbye. The Protestant thing, again, although at the time it was exactly what I needed for a clean break. They got in the car and drove off. I headed up to my room, alone but not lonely.

Through the years, I stayed in touch and heard from our dad occasionally. He even sent a care package with snacks and miniature bottles of booze to share with my freshman roommates.

Our calls usually went something like: "O.K., now, can we go over the kids' birthdays again? I'll write them all down this time so I don't forget any!"

In college, I came to realize just how extensive the money gap is in America and how different my experience was as a kid growing up in Racine. First, a lot of kids didn't have to work a couple of jobs to pay for school. Second, they seemed to have a leisurely approach to school and studied as if there were no concern about losing scholarship money (because a lot of them didn't have to worry about that). Eventually, it became clear to me that most of the students were from backgrounds very different from mine.

Once, when visiting my college roommate's parents in Carmel, Indiana, over spring break, I was awestruck by everything: the size of the house, the cleanliness of everything, the foreign cars. The house was massive and new, and looked like the type of home where all the plumbing, lighting, and heating actually worked. It had central air that was on all the time. A Jack-and-Jill bathroom was upstairs.

When I peeked into the linen closet out of curiosity in that room, I could not believe what I saw: hundreds and hundreds of dollars' worth of cleaning and personal supplies of every kind. Shampoo, conditioner, hair spray, tissues, swabs, bandages, nail polish remover, air fresheners, soaps. Everything. They had backups. Backups.

Back at our townhome in Georgetown, everything was purchased on a week-to-week basis. We didn't have the money to buy things in advance and barely got what we needed every week on our mom's waitress salary.

Fast-forward to college. I was jealous, but mostly, I was in awe. Other people had so much. Other people had so many opportunities. Other people could pay their bills. They didn't worry about groceries or insurance or any of the countless things that stressed out our mom and the rest of us after our parents' divorce, when our dad bounced from job to job with stints of no income whatsoever.

Whatever the differences or shortcomings or disappointments, eventually, those who leave get to the point in life where they want to simply find a way to get back home. Wisconsin is insufferably cold at times, that is true. But it is a sensible, predictable, and beautiful place filled with interesting people from North and South, Denmark, Germany, Mexico, Greece, and other places all over the world.

For me, a few years in Miami, Florida, followed by two decades as an attorney in Chicago, meant it was time. The trees, the lakes, the food, and well above and beyond all, the people of Wisconsin, kept calling. Wisconsin is a place where people can live through twenty-one straight days of crappy, cold gray weather without falling apart. Its residents endure eight months of static electricity, cracking dry hands, and cold toilet seats through the fall, winter, and spring, and still greet you with a smile on the street. People generally consider themselves accountable for their actions, work hard, and don't expect the world to rise up to take on every problem for them without a chip on their shoulder.

In the Midwest, there are four very distinct seasons and its people are able to clearly keep track of time and events without operating under some sort of misconception that time is standing still. No mistake can be made that its residents are not aging because unlike warmer climates, one season will never imperceptibly flow into another as though time were standing still.

Trees, grasses, and flowers change as the earth makes its way around the sun and Mother Nature gives her best. Every autumn, she takes the opportunity to show off by way of a natural fireworks display of trees changing in every possible combination of colors imaginable. Leaves of crimson, orange, and gold fall from the trees while evergreens hold their ground over the bitter cold winter with its frost, snowstorms, and unbelievably fresh air. Spring follows with bursts of green and wildflowers picking up where they left off the prior year. The passage of time can be specifically tracked and that is perfectly fine.

Children from all parts of the world may grow up in more predictable environments free from socio-economic disadvantages. Those who do not generally have a way of finding outlets, whether through nature, school, older siblings, or even friends, to make life better. A person can bear very little resentment at the end of the day for childhoods that don't quite measure up to what they may have wanted or expected. Parents and other people do the best they can. We almost never know or understand the struggles past or present in the mind of another. We can screw things up perfectly well on our own, and don't need a family or a mom or dad to blame for everything we don't like about our lives or ourselves.

If it hasn't been written yet, there ought to be a book titled *I'm all f*cked up, and it's all my fault*. Living through less-than-perfect experiences provides lessons. If we're lucky, we take these experiences out with us in the world as part of a toolbox to help us understand and get along with the rest of the inhabitants of the world we encounter. If we're really lucky, we use them to raise children who grow up to be people who are better than us in a million little ways.

Epilogue

As I write, our dad has been gone for almost two decades. He never slept much and seemed to have a ton of energy for a guy who had a big belly he referred to as his "Irish Tumor" caused by little exercise and good times, which included a steady diet of too much fun and little care about tomorrow. He'd try to get us out of bed on those early school-day mornings by singing or telling us to "Sleep when you're dead!" He had a point. He also used to tell us: "There's something wrong with every single one of us." He usually told us this when we were talking poorly about someone else. It was a nicer way of telling us: "You're not perfect." He was right.

It's as though he knew his time on earth wouldn't be particularly long and he used every minute on earth as well as he could, within his own set of limitations, much like the rest of us.

Our brother John, who had more talent and potential than the lot of us, passed away at age 52 due to the combined effects of crippling alcoholism and terribly poor nutrition, a great irony considering he was a cook and was around food all the time. He ate nothing that had any color to it. John went for the all-white part of holiday meals: turkey breast, mashed potatoes- no gravy, white rolls.

Our mom, on the other hand, is still a force to be reckoned with at the age of 82. Forty years of smoking and diets ruled by Slim-fast and Dexatrim diet pills in the presence of little to no exercise, be damned. Hard work. A decent draw from the gene pool and years of challenges that seemed to make her even tougher as time went on. In a way, she had the indomitable spirit of those miners digging caves in their newly adopted Badger State.

* * *

Special thanks to my early readers and supporters, especially Tim and Margie, who always looked out for me, even when they couldn't be there.

Thanks to Kira Henschel for her thoughts, feedback, and help in getting this book across the finish line.

Thanks to every teacher I ever had, especially the ones who loved teaching, including Mr. Worden at Case High School and Dr. Bruno Schlessinger at Saint Mary's College. Your love of teaching showed.

Thanks to my birth mother, Pam Goodman Hickey, who found me when I most needed it.

And thanks to our mom, Jackie, who worked hard most of her adult life to do the best she could for her family.

Finally, thank you to my core group, my team, my best people: John, Isabel, Michael, and Caroline. My whole heart and whole being love you, more than you will ever know.

CPSIA information can be obtained
at www.ICGtesting.com
Printed in the USA
FSHW020511061120
75654FS